Paper Safe

*The triumph of bureaucracy in
safety management*

Gregory Smith

I want a job where I don't spend endless hours circulating information that isn't relevant about subjects that don't matter to people who aren't interested. I want a job where there is achievement rather than merely activity. I'm tired of pushing paper.
(Lynn & Jay, 1984)

Contents

Introduction 1

A word about case studies 5

A word about case citations 11

A word about the trivial 12

The infinite regression of supervision 15

Part 1 22

What is bureaucracy and why does it matter? 22

What is Bureaucracy? 23

Rules 32

The handrail conundrum 40

Bureaucracy or Complexity? 46

The Safety Paradox 52

The illusion of safety 58

One-Off Departure or Systemic Failure 65

Part 2 69

Bureaucracy in action 69

General 70

Who are you writing for? 83

Audits and accreditation 87

Training and competence 93

Workplace tools 98

Incident investigations 120

Health and safety reporting 132

Part 3 139

Where to from here? 139

Managing legal risk 140

Understand if your systems are useful 147

Connection with purpose 149

Critically question health and safety reports 155

Incident investigations 158

Final thoughts 161

References 164

Gregory Smith

INTRODUCTION

I n 2014, a client asked me to come into their office and speak to several senior managers about their obligations for safety and health. During our reasonably informal discussions, I made the observation that one of the biggest barriers to managers understanding and discharging their obligations for safety and health was the extraordinary bureaucracy and largely impenetrable language characterising health and safety management systems. These discussions inspired one of the managers – a senior commercial position – to go away and read some of their safety management procedures.

His observation?

Unintelligible Gobbledygook

The sentiment is not new and has been expressed in accident inquiries over decades, although, with respect to my client, somewhat more eloquently.

On 2 September 2006, RAF Nimrod XV230 was on a routine mission over Helmand Province in Southern Afghanistan in support of NATO and Afghani ground forces when she suffered a catastrophic mid-air fire, leading to the loss of the aircraft and the death of everyone on board.

On 4 December 2007, the then UK Secretary of State for Defence announced a review into the disaster (Haddon-Cave, 2009). The Terms of Reference for the review included:

> *To examine the arrangements for assuring the airworthiness and safe operation of the Nimrod MR2 in the period from its introduction in 1979 to the accident on 2 September 2006, including hazard analysis, the safety case compiled in 2005, maintenance arrangements, and responses to any earlier incidents which might have highlighted the risk and led to corrective action;*

And

> *To assess more broadly the process for compiling safety cases, taking account of best practice in the civilian and military world;* (Haddon-Cave, 2009, p. 6)

The safety management systems in that case were described as follows:

> *The current MOD Airworthiness system is of Byzantine complexity* (Haddon-Cave, 2009, p. 41).

The purpose of this book is to highlight bureaucracy in health and safety management, why it is a problem, how it arises and to suggest some solutions, some ways to de-clutter health and safety management. I strongly believe less bureaucracy and more clarity will benefit health and safety management. It will help health and safety management because people will have a better understanding of what they are expected to do, and management will have a better understanding about whether the health and safety risks in their businesses are being managed.

At the same time, I am not arguing change for the sake of change.

Gregory Smith

My basic premise is:

- Safety management can become too bureaucratic to work effectively.

- Bureaucracy hides the true state of safety and creates an illusion safety is well managed, when it is not.

- Much of what we do in the name of safety management, especially the bureaucracy and administration, is unnecessary and ineffective – it adds nothing to the "*safety*" of workplaces.

- Bureaucracy makes life harder for workers and more difficult for them to understand the health and safety risks in the workplace.

- Bureaucracy distracts organisations, so they do not pay proper attention to what they *say they do* in the name of health and safety. They do not analyse their information and they do not know if their health and safety initiatives "*work*".

While my personal perspective is built around safety management in Australia, the issues of bureaucracy described in this book appear to have global application. Indeed, they seem to be consistent around the world. Moreover, the observations in this book are likely to have application beyond health and safety. Management systems more generally, for example environmental, human resources and so on, all seem to be infected with the same bureaucratic triumph.

It is certainly the case that investigations into major accidents everywhere on the planet find similar concerns about the level of bureaucracy in safety management and the impact this has in workplaces.

As with everything I write about health and safety, this book is not a definitive answer, nor is it an "*all seeing all knowing*" analysis of every safety management system everywhere. What it is, I hope, is a thoughtful analysis of cases and history that give organisations pause for thought about their safety management and the way they approach health and safety in their workplaces.

Gregory Smith

A WORD ABOUT CASE STUDIES

I have used a lot of case studies in this book, because I believe they are the best way to illustrate the points I am trying to make. However, case studies do have limitations.

The first type of *"case study"* I use, are my experiences from working with clients. Obviously, these observations are personal, subjective, and influenced by my own biases.

As far as possible, I have tried to place my experiences alongside published research, inquiries, reports, and cases. I have done this to try and illustrate that my experiences are consistent with published information about workplace accidents. I also believe this shows that the systemic failures of safety management we see when workplace accidents are *publicly* reported, are far more common and prevalent then we might think. Systemic failures in safety management can exist quite happily for many years without an accident.

The second type of case study I use are inquiries – most often major accident inquiries and coroners' reports.

These types of inquiries are very useful to help us understand safety management systems *in practice*, because typically, the inquiry has wide ranging terms of reference to understand *"why"* accidents happen and make recommendations about preventing future occurrences. An inquiry will have a broad remit, which allows it to go beyond the specific circumstances of an accident and look at safety management more holistically, including external influences such as regulators, economic pressure and so on.

In my experience, inquiries provide the best framework to understand safety management holistically and get a sense of how complex and interconnected safety management can be.

Finally, I have referred extensively to prosecutions under health and safety legislation.

These legal cases are helpful to understand the *"boundaries"* that apply to safety management. How far do you have to go to provide safe systems of work?

However, reported prosecutions do have real limitations in understanding safety management.

Prosecutions are not concerned with safety management per se. Prosecutions are concerned with the *"particulars"* of the charge against the defendant.

In a prosecution, the prosecutor alleges that a defendant has failed to do something – for example, failed to manage hazards in the workplace as far as *"reasonably practicable"*. The argument in a prosecution is not whether the defendant had safe systems of work, but rather, whether the prosecution can prove beyond a reasonable doubt the defendant failed to manage a particular hazard as far as reasonably practicable.

This structure creates some anomalies that people who are not familiar with the prosecution process find strange.

Legally, it is possible to have unsafe systems of work but to have managed a hazard *"as low as reasonably practicable"* in the context of a specific charge or a specific, particularised, breach of health and safety legislation. Reasonably practicable, is not the same as *"everything possible"* and just because something can be done which might improve safety, does not mean it has to be done (see for example *Baiada Poultry Pty Ltd v The Queen* [2012] HCA 14, [33]).

First, the law is quite clear; employers do not have to prevent all accidents. Employers only need take the steps set out in health and safety legislation. Complying with health and safety legislation is not always the same as preventing accident:

> *The Act does not require employers to ensure that accidents never happen. It requires them to take such steps as are practicable to provide and maintain a safe working environment.* (See for example: Holmes v Re Spence & Co Pty Ltd (1992) 5 VIR 119, 123 – 124; Laing O'Rourke (BMC) Pty Ltd v Kirwin [2011] WASCA 117 [31]).

Second, a defendant can breach their obligations even if their failure does not cause or contribute to an accident. Indeed, a defendant can breach their obligations even if there is no accident:

> *Crucially, the prosecution does not need to prove that the employer's breach 'caused' the accident, or that the taking of particular safety measures would have changed the course of events on the day in question. Put another way, the prosecution does not need to establish that the defendant employer should have anticipated the risk of events unfolding precisely as they did on the day of the fatal accident.*

As we have said, proof that the alleged breach caused the death (or injury) is not an element of the offence charged. On the contrary, as explained in the reasons which follow, the prosecution need only establish that:

(c) (sic) there was a risk to employee health and safety;

(d) the measures identified as necessary would have eliminated or reduced the risk (as the case may be); and

(e) it was 'reasonably practicable' in the circumstances for the employer to have taken those measures.

(See: DPP v Vibro-Pile (Aust) Pty Ltd [2016] VSCA 55, [5] – [6].)

This is an important issue in the context of bureaucracy, because an employer can be found liable for not enforcing their own systems of work (i.e. the bureaucracy) even though the failure of the "*system of work*", did not cause or contribute to the accident. We will look at this issue later in the book.

Finally, prosecutions are limited to the allegations made against a defendant. This can result in a curious situation whereby an employer might be "*not guilty*" of the allegations against them, even though the case reveals failures of safety management which could otherwise give rise to a conviction.

For example, in *Workcover Authority of New South Wales (Inspector Byer) v Cleary Bros (Bombo)* Pty Ltd [2001] NSWIRComm 278, a worker was injured while unloading a truck at a waste collection facility. The worker slipped and fell into a pit which was about 1.8 metres deep. As result of the fall, the worker suffered serious head injuries, a broken rib, two broken wrists, as well as bruising and swelling.

The allegations against Defendant were:

- They did not install barriers to ensure a person could not fall into the pit; and

- They did not ensure the floor next to the pit was clean and free of debris.

The Court found Defendant not guilty of the charges, saying:

> *I do not consider that it was reasonably practicable for the defendant to address the failings identified in the prosecutor's case. The prosecutor's case was limited to allegations that the defendant failed to provide an effective barrier and failed to ensure that the area was clean and free of debris. On the evidence before the Court, I am satisfied that the defendant has discharged its onus of proving that it was not reasonably practicable either to erect an effective barrier on the side of the pit catering for mechanically unloading vehicles or to ensure that the area beside the pit was always clean and free of debris so as to ensure that a person could not slip and fall.* [99]

However, at the end of the case the Court also made the following observation:

> *Whilst it is not the position of the Court to specify what measures were required, it is possible that there were failings in effective supervision, adequate warnings or in the condition of the ground (even aside from the metal plates) that gave rise to the risk. **These were not matters that were alleged as part of the prosecution.*** (my emphasis added) [100].

This observation highlights one of the weaknesses inherent in prosecutions as a tool for safety improvement. The prosecution is limited to its charges – it is limited to its allegations about what might have been reasonably practicable.

While the prosecution could not prove it was reasonably practicable to erect the relevant barriers and keep the work area clean, there may have been other measures the employer could have taken to prevent the incident. However, the prosecution did not raise these "*other measures*" in the case.

Despite the limitations in different case studies, in their defence, they do offer useful insights into safety management. In my experience, the challenge is to focus on what can be learned and applied, rather than what is missing or might not make sense.

Also, and I hope it becomes obvious throughout the course of this book, the case studies I discuss have something to say about health and safety bureaucracy – even if they do not use that term. The case studies show how health and safety bureaucracy can undermine health and safety management, compromise legal compliance and work against the objectives of the organisation. If nothing else, the case studies should encourage us to challenge, proactively and consciously, what we do in the name of health and safety to understand whether it adds value to safety outcomes, or merely adds to a growing volume of distraction.

A WORD ABOUT CASE CITATIONS

I have cited several legal cases throughout this book which you can find at the Australasian Legal Information Institute website, www.austlii.edu.au. The website offers free access to Australian case law, legislation and other material, and while you are there I encourage you to contribute to the site to help them continue their work.

For people who are not familiar with legal case citations, you will often see a reference to a number in square brackets, for example:

> *the phrase "reasonably practicable" means something narrower than "physically possible" or "feasible".* [53]

The number is a reference to the paragraph number which will help you find the referenced text most easily.

A WORD ABOUT THE TRIVIAL

A common criticism of health and safety is the extent it seems to focus on the trivial. An obvious example of this is health and safety's seeming obsession with personal injury rates as a measure of safety performance. They are not, but I will discuss injury rates and other forms of health and safety reporting later in the book.

Over and above injury reporting, however, there are many examples of apparently trivial health and safety requirements being enforced in workplaces. Common examples I encounter include:

- Banning knives in workplaces;

- Constant reminders to hold handrails;

- Ongoing admonishment to always cross the road at traffic lights;

- Warnings about hot water being "*hot*"; or

- Requiring lids on coffee cups when walking around the office with hot coffee.

Gregory Smith

I was once in a client's office and had to use the bathroom. Having done what I needed to do, I washed my hands and when I went to use the paper towel to dry them, I notice a *"warning"* on the paper towel dispenser:

Caution: sharp edges

Presumably, this was a reference to the nasty serrated edges I had to navigate to access the paper towel.

I have no doubt people could easily give more example of trivial health and safety requirements in their workplaces. Indeed, naming and shaming trivial health and safety rules is a favourite pastime for critics of health and safety. However, the fact a health and safety requirement might seem to be trivial does not make it bureaucratic.

Trivial health and safety requirements can undermine health and safety in several ways.

They may contribute to *"initiative overload"*.

They may contribute to the *"illusion of safety"*.

Trivial health and safety requirements are very likely to disengage your workforce from your safety message and create a perception that all health and safety requirements are trivial nonsense.

But none of these things mean trivial matters are bureaucratic, at least not in the sense I am using the term in this book. In my view, there is an important distinction between trivial and bureaucratic.

Dealing with trivial health and safety rules and managing bureaucracy are two different issues. Rules may be trivial, but in most cases, they have some connection to their purpose. A rule to hold the handrail because we do not want you to fall down the stairs, whatever you might have to say as a functioning adult about that rule, nevertheless serves a purpose – and the purpose and the rule are inextricably linked.

Bureaucracy is different. The problem with bureaucracy is that it has lost its connection with purpose. A pre-start checklist for a piece of equipment may or may not be trivial, but when the predominant purpose of the checklist is to meet a key performance indicator or provide evidence that 100% of pre-start checklists have been done in a monthly health and safety report, then the process has become bureaucratic. The process is no longer connected to the purpose of ensuring safe vehicles – or at least not in the minds of the people who are completing the checklist.

I do not want to suggest that trivial health and safety requirements and bureaucracy are mutually exclusive, and they can often feed off one another. But I think it is important to recognise that doing away with trivial health and safety requirements in the workplace will not necessarily make health and safety less bureaucratic, and it will not necessarily contribute to a clearer picture of health and safety.

THE INFINITE REGRESSION OF SUPERVISION

Organisations often feel morally obliged to do everything they can for safety.

While this may be a laudable objective and doing everything you can in the name of health and safety cannot, of itself be criticised, we must always recognise that just because we do something in the name of health and safety does not mean it improves health and safety outcomes. We should always consider health and safety initiatives and how we implement them, being very conscious of the limitations posed by the Safety Paradox and the Illusion of Safety, both of which I discuss later in the book.

Notwithstanding the "*moral imperatives*" for health and safety and the desire to do everything possible, the law in Australia and many other jurisdictions demands something less. An employer's obligations to manage health and safety are bounded by, and limited to, doing everything "*reasonably practicable*".

I do not intend to discuss reasonably practicable in detail in this book, except to say that understanding the limits of our obligations may give us confidence to tackle issues around bureaucracy in health and safety management.

Consistent with the limitations of reasonably practicable, we have already seen in the discussion about case studies, the law does not require employers to prevent all accidents (See for example: *Holmes v Re Spence & Co Pty Ltd* (1992) 5 VIR 119, 123 – 124; *Laing O'Rourke (BMC) Pty Ltd v Kirwin* [2011] WASCA 117 [31]).

Similarly, the law does not need an employer to do everything "*possible*" to prevent accidents. In the High Court decision, *Slivak v Lurgi (Australia) Pty Ltd* [2001] HCA 6, Justice Gaudron noted:

> *the phrase "reasonably practicable" means something narrower than "physically possible" or "feasible".* [53]

We can see the practical implications of this principle in a case like *Inspector Davies v Prospect Electricity* (unreported, Fisher P, CT747, 9 Nov 1992). In the case, a linesman and lineworker started working on high-voltage electric power lines without waiting for an access permit confirming that the lines were isolated. There was an electrical explosion killing one of the workers, the other was seriously injured.

The prosecution alleged one of the failings of the employer was a lack of supervision. In response to the allegation, the Court said:

> *It is a version of the infinite regression of supervision argument, which if accepted would mean that every well trained tradesman should be supervised or observed by a superior trained tradesman, and he seemingly in turn should be supervised himself by someone even higher.*
>
> *The 'lack of instruction' submission relied upon founders on the same practical argument. No fully trained and experienced tradesman needs to be told to cross the road*

16

safely, or to be accompanied by a supervisor to ensure that he does so. Similarly, a thoroughly trained and qualified tradesman, employed after extensive instruction, the adequacy of which again is not criticised, does not need to be advised not to grasp an unprotected wire energised by 11KCV, nor in the real world, should supervisors be on stand by in case he does.

...

... that the sole cause of the accident was that through some inexplicable inadvertence the two men did not attend to a safe system of work which they had undoubtedly been thoroughly taught and for many years had consistently followed, which failure led directly to a fatal accident which was in the full sense of the word, an accident. No other explanation would appear to be available.

If we accept, as discussed earlier, one of the limitations of prosecutions as case studies is we do not know everything about the circumstances of the accident, given the prosecution focuses on particular charges we can, nevertheless, think about this case in the context of health and safety bureaucracy.

In particular, one of the *"go to"* reactions of health and safety following an accident is to *"layer"* the work practice with more bureaucracy – additional training, added checklists and more procedure.

A legitimate question in these circumstances is, if the process we had to manage the relevant hazard – working on high-voltage power lines – did not work in this case, how would adding more process improve things? If an accident has occurred because workers ignore our process, is more process really the thing which will get them to pay attention?

Another example comes out of a series of prosecutions in Western Australia which were known as the *"Cyclone George"* cases.

In March 2007, Cyclone George crossed the coast north east of Port Headland in the Pilbara region of Western Australia. At the time, Fortescue Metals Group and several contractors and subsidiary companies were building a railway line between iron ore mining and processing facilities run by Fortescue at their Cloudbreak Mine in the Pilbara and port facilities at Port Hedland.

At that time, entities involved in constructing the railway line were staying at a construction village, known as "Rail Camp 1", which was made up primarily of residential units known as *"dongas"*. Rail Camp 1 had been constructed by another company, NT Link.

There were a range of technical issues in the case about the location of the Rail Camp, the way the dongas had been constructed and whether the dongas were properly "rated" for the cyclone region where they were situated. When Cyclone George came through the Rail Camp, the winds dislodged the concrete footings of some of the dongas, and some of the steel tie rods holding the dongas in place were pulled free, causing some dongas to lift and pull away from their foundations. Some blew against other dongas. Some were overturned.

Several employees were seriously injured, and there were some fatalities.

There were several companies prosecuted as a result of the incident. The cases are very instructive on *"reasonably practicable"* and the relationship between principals and contractors in the context of health and safety. However, the cases also add to the discussion about the infinite regression of supervision.

In *Laing O'Rourke (BMC) Pty Ltd v Kirwin* [2011] WASCA 117, the prosecution alleged that the dongas were not safe because they had not been designed to withstand cyclonic forces in the region, and their construction was defective. The prosecution said the employer should not have made any *"assumptions"* about the suitability of the dongas.

The case was initially appealed to the Supreme Court (*Kirwin v Laing O'Rourke (BMC) Pty Ltd* [2010] WASC 194), where the Court said the employer should have made its own inquiries, including getting independent engineering advice about whether the dongas had been properly designed and built.

When the matter was heard in the full Court of the Supreme Court (*Laing O'Rourke (BMC) Pty Ltd v Kirwin* [2011] WASCA 117), the Court said:

> *In my respectful view, by concluding that the appellant was required to carry out its own inquiries and investigations, including by obtaining engineering advice, into the design and fabrication of the dongas for the purpose of assessing their suitability for cyclonic conditions, his Honour ascribed a content to the duty under s 19 which went beyond what was reasonably practicable in the circumstances. [67]*
>
> *...*
>
> *Nor was there anything to suggest that a reasonable employer in the position of the appellant would have appreciated or foreseen that the accommodation was not properly designed and built to withstand the weather conditions that affect the area in which it was located, or that it otherwise posed a risk of injury in the event of a cyclone. The donga accommodation was understood to have been built for a reputable and competent organisation with good quality control, and to have met the requirements of the local authority, including in*

relation to building standards for cyclone-affected areas. [68]

Chief Justice Martin noted:

... the effect of the judge's conclusion was that every contractor whose employee spent any time in the camp would be obliged to receive engineering advice of an unspecified kind and undertake engineering investigations of an unspecified nature of all the dongas in the camp in order to discharge the statutory obligation imposed by the legislation. Because the camp was not under the control of those contractors, it would be necessary for each contractor to secure the right to conduct such investigations as a condition of the placement of any employee in the camp. [4]

Further, the reasoning of the judge could tend to suggest that every employer placing an employee in any accommodation for any period of time in any area of Australia which is at risk of cyclonic winds would have a similar obligation to take engineering advice of an unspecified kind and undertake engineering investigations of an unspecified nature in respect of every building in which any employee was accommodated. A duty of that kind would be plainly impracticable. [5]

While I can understand some people's objections to the observations in this section, they are not in any way intended to downplay the importance of health and safety management, nor the very high obligations that health and safety legislation imposes on employers to manage health and safety risk in the business.

However, much of what is done in the name of health and safety – particularly the bureaucracy – is sold to organisations in the name of legal compliance. What I hope has emerged in this book

20

already, and what I will continue to emphasise throughout the book is:

- Health and safety bureaucracy does not necessarily add to improved health and safety outcomes;

- In many cases, health and is a bureaucracy is not a legal requirement and does not add to legal compliance; and

- Often, health and safety bureaucracy undermine health and safety performance and at the same time compromises legal compliance. In many cases, health and safety bureaucracy is the biggest source of legal liability.

These are things that I will continue to explore in the rest of the book.

PART 1
WHAT IS
BUREAUCRACY AND
WHY DOES IT
MATTER?

WHAT IS BUREAUCRACY?

S top me if you have heard this one before.

An organisation is about to introduce a new hazard reporting process and they want to make sure it gets "*traction*". To help embed the process, they introduce a "*quota*" system, or "*Key Performance Indicator*". Everyone (i.e. the workers) must produce one hazard report a shift, they will be handed in, counted, collated and reported to site management using a "*traffic light*" dashboard. A "*green*" traffic light means more than 95% compliance with the requirement, in other words more than 95% of the workers have produced their hazard report for each shift. Amber means 65% – 95% compliance, and red means less than 65% compliance with the process.

Thankfully for all concerned, the health and safety reports are consistently green, and everybody is comfortable (using very tenuous logic and unjustifiable assumptions) that the workers on site are identifying hazards associated with their tasks.

The relationship between the number of hazard reports done and the understanding of hazards is of course a non sequitur. What the green traffic light does not tell you, amongst many things, is:

- How many hazard reports were done in the lunchroom without any regard to the actual state of the workplace?

- How many hazard reports were done on the bus on the way to work?

- How many hazard reports were done in the pub on Sunday night?

The reality, of course, is that the "*number*" of hazard reports done tells us nothing about their quality. It tells us nothing about the efficacy of safety management.

None of this is news, or a mystery. Health and safety management on site is content with the process. They know it does not add any real value or insight, but if people (i.e. again, the workers) can get into the habit of doing hazard reports – if we focus on the quantity we will eventually train people and focus on quality. Once the process is embedded!

Except that never happens.

Hazard reporting remains a metric exercise, where the number (especially the green traffic light) has far more value – indeed they become the only measure of value – that any possible insight into the real hazards in the workplace.

There is, with some justification, criticism about safety management systems and how they are applied in practice. Indeed, this book is filled with examples of how safety management systems, especially *documented* safety management systems can undermine good safety management and create, not reduce, legal risk. Most often, this criticism is couched in the language of volume and complexity – there is too much "*stuff*", and it is too difficult to know what to do. In this context, people are most critical of "*rules*". There are too many rules. Rules deal with trivial matters, not the important safety issues. The rules are too hard for people to understand, and on it goes.

Certainly, we can find these elements in safety management and they can be problematic.

However, we need to be cautious because bureaucracy is not just about volume and complexity – although they can be a by-product of bureaucracy. We need to understand the challenge of bureaucracy, recognising it is more than just a move from "*complexity*" to "*simplicity*".

Systems can be voluminous and complex without being bureaucratic.

Systems can also be bureaucratic while being simple and sparse.

Systems can be bureaucratic without being documented, although I grant you, most bureaucratic systems are characterised by high levels of documentation.

Let me illustrate the differences with some examples.

I am aware of a company with operations on the east coast of Australia which include maintenance operations in a high hazard industry. As part of their "*system*", they have a uniform policy. The company has a winter and summer uniform. Workers must wear the winter uniform after 31 March, and the summer uniform after 30 September. The rule is strictly applied, regardless of climatic conditions on the "*changeover*" date.

To me, this is classic bureaucracy; a triumph of form over substance, of process over purpose.

A rule to have a winter and summer uniform does not have to be bureaucratic in the sense I am using it. However, when the rule becomes arbitrary, triggered by a date regardless of weather conditions (the hazard it is trying to manage) then, in my view, it is bureaucratic.

Bureaucracy is not the same thing as rules. Some rules can be straight forward and discretionary. They are not arbitrary. They do not substantially impact on how work is performed, and do not require paperwork, planning and approval.

However, even straightforward rules can become bureaucratic.

Like most children in Australia, I was brought up with some education about road safety, but it was not until I started working in the oil and gas industry in the late 1990s when I became aware crossing the road at traffic lights was actually a "*workplace*" rule

I have no doubt many people find their employer routinely reminding them to cross the street at a set of traffic lights trivial, unnecessary or even insulting. I know I did. However, looking back on the "*rule*" there is a level of tension in the workplace context which an employer has to manage, and I discuss this later in the book when I talk about the "*handrail conundrum*" – I understand the need for the rule. A rule to always cross the road at a set of traffic lights – in itself – would not be bureaucratic in the sense I am using it in this book.

A requirement to do a risk assessment and find the best place to cross the road and have the risk assessment approved by a supervisor before crossing the road and have a certain percentage of those risk assessments independently reviewed, would be bureaucratic.

Gregory Smith

In my experience, we can see whether processes or systems are bureaucratic in several ways. Often, the process or system becomes excessive and out of all proportion to the goal it is trying to achieve, in fact no one even remembers the goal. Like my crossing the road example above. Often, this deteriorates to the point where the process or system is counter-productive to the goal.

For me, the most significant, and damaging, marker of bureaucracy is when process becomes more important than purpose. When the process, or more precisely compliance with the process, becomes a measure of success, instead of the "*purpose*" of the process. This is evident in the uniform example above: The measure of success has become compliance with the changeover date, not protection from climatic conditions.

We can also see an example of "*process over purpose*" bureaucracy in training and competence for health and safety.

Training and competence is an essential element of effective safety management, and health and safety legislation mandates training as a key element of an employer's obligations to provide safe workplaces. For example, the *Model Work Health and Safety Act* (section 19) says the employer must ensure, "*so far as is reasonably practicable*":

> *the provision of any information, training, instruction or supervision that is necessary to protect all persons from risks to their health and safety arising from work carried out as part of the conduct of the business or undertaking; and*

Different people will no doubt have different ways to describe the "*goal*" of "*training*" in the context of health and safety. The precise characterisation of the goal is not especially important for this discussion, but I will simply frame it as ensuring workers understand the health and safety hazards associated with the work they perform.

The difficulty, in my experience, is that organisations do not measure, or look to clarify this level of *"understanding"*. Instead, organisations measure health and safety training by *"activity"*, for example, the percentage of training completed against a training schedule.

Paperwork dominates training in health and safety, characterised by ensuring adequate attendance lists, making sure people have *"signed on"* to training and tracking training attendance in a database.

However, none of these matters – these processes – are conclusive of effective training. At best, these processes show training was *"done"*. To be effective, and legally defendable, training must be:

a. Done;

b. Understood;

c. Implemented in the workplace; and

d. Enforced/reinforced.

Whatever your approach to training for health and safety, the ultimate test of its efficacy is the level of *understanding* and how workers apply it in *practice* – not the process of training or compliance with the process, and there are many examples which illustrate this in practice. I have summarised some examples below.

Case	Summary of training	Outcome
Harris v Coles Supermarkets Australia Pty Ltd [2017] ACTSC 81	Video and face to face training with documented checklists signed by workers confirming they understood. Hazards not understood.	More than $1 million in damages awarded to an injured employee.

Inspector Shepherd v Desiya Pty Ltd [2013] NSWIRComm 9	Training not documented. Buddy system used. No evidence of comprehension or understanding of the hazards.	Convicted of breaches of health and safety legislation.
Safe Work NSW v Wollongong Glass P/L [2016] NSWDC 58	Training not documented. Buddy system used. Defendant could show evidence of comprehension and understanding of the hazards	Acquitted of breaches of health and safety legislation
Moore v SD Tillett Memorials Pty Ltd [2013] SAIRC 47	System not documented, but hazards and correct system of work understood by the workers.	Acquitted of breaches of health and safety legislation
Fry v Keating [2013] WASCA 109	System not documented, and hazards and correct system of work not understood by the workers.	Convicted of breaches of health and safety legislation

In each case it was the level of comprehension and understanding – the *outcome*, the *"purpose"* - not the process or compliance with it, which drove the result.

It is here we can see the influence of bureaucracy on health and safety management. For many organisations, the structure and measure of health and safety training is wholly bureaucratic, driven by compliance with the process with little or no regard for the purpose, in this case, to ensure understanding.

If you think this is an overly harsh observation, test it in your own organisation. Look at how you measure training. Is it a measure of activity? Are your performance indicators for training driven by compliance to a schedule? What information is available to you, and what reports give insight into whether training in the organisation delivers the level of understanding it was designed to achieve? Is there any evidence your training processes achieve the purpose for which they were designed?

Another way bureaucracy in safety management has been described is by differentiating between *"prescription"* and *"discretion"*. Opponents of current approaches to safety management often argue for more discretion for workers in how they perform their work.

My earlier example about winter and summer uniforms could be argued in support of this position. It does seem perfectly reasonable to say that workers should have a *"discretion"* about what uniform they wear, depending on the weather at any given time. Again however, we need to be a little bit cautious in our thinking – it is not an *"all or nothing game"*. I believe there are perfectly sound reasons for supporting more discretion for workers and how they perform their work, but we should not regard safety management as bureaucratic, simply because it is prescriptive. I accept that prescription can be a characteristic of bureaucracy, but only, in my view, to the extent it is not *"connected to purpose"*.

In the uniform example, if the purpose of having a summer and winter uniform is to have the best – *"safest"* – uniform for climatic conditions and you want to make that a prescriptive requirement, then you prescribe the relevant climatic conditions (i.e. above/below a certain temperature or UV index) – you link prescription to purpose. Arguably, linking a change of uniform to a fixed date is more about the ease of policing and enforcement, rather than safety. Indeed, this type of bureaucratic prescription seems to hold true for Personal Protective Equipment (PPE).

Think about hardhats. For many organisations it is much easier to mandate the use of hardhats whenever you go outside, rather than describe a set of conditions – risk related conditions – when they must be worn. It is just easier to police and enforce a blanket rule rather than a set of risk criteria.

In my view, when prescription becomes disconnected from any genuine purpose and its only real outcome is to make the administration process easier, then it crosses into bureaucracy.

RULES

A lot of what people perceive to be wrong with safety is the plethora of *"rules"*. But rules are not bureaucratic per se.

I recall my very first trip to an offshore gas producing platform. I was outside in the evening watching the sun go down over the ocean, and the mass of sea life that was accumulating underneath the light from the flare. I found it a fascinating and beautiful experience.

Not knowing any better, I quite naturally started taking photographs of what was happening around me.

I had not considered, even for a second, the possibility that taking photographs with my little digital camera presented some sort of safety risk. At least not until a very large, tobacco chewing Texan pointed it out to me.

Beyond personal embarrassment, I did not think too much of the incident at the time. However, on reflection based on the intervening 20 years of experience, there were several interesting aspects to what occurred.

First, I think the incident says something about the effectiveness of the organisation's induction processes. I know I was inducted, I just obviously did not learn anything from the process.

Second, the incident also says something about the importance, or otherwise, of safety – or at least this particular rule – for the organisation. The person who pulled me up for breaching the rule had, apparently, been watching me take photographs for a good five or 10 minutes before stopping me, so obviously the issue was not too urgent. Moreover, as far as I was aware no investigation was ever done into this breach to understand why a young lawyer could roam freely on an production platform taking photographs.

But for all that, it is clear that rules serve a purpose. People do not have an inherent understanding of risks in their workplace, let alone in workplaces they are not familiar with. Rules are not bureaucratic in their own right and do not necessarily undermine health and safety.

In seeking to shift safety management from bureaucracy to clarity, we must be careful not to diminish things that are truly valuable.

In my mind, there is no doubt we need rules in workplaces to manage health and safety risks. Much of what we know today about managing health and safety risks – our rules – we have learned from the suffering of others, and it would be tragic and stupid to let those lessons be lost.

However, rules are on a continuum.

At one end we have rules which are very important. Often, they are rules which help us understand critical risks.

Very often, rules help make clear hazards which might otherwise be hidden.

At the other end of the continuum, we find rules which people perceive as ridiculous and trivial, and I have touched on examples of these earlier.

Along the continuum we find rules which are relevant to a hazard but frustrate people because they relate to activities people navigate perfectly well outside of work and find them silly in the workplace. People believe they have enough life experience to manage these hazards and exercise their own judgement and discretion.

Sometimes, rules do become a problem in organisations (see for example Dekker, 2015, Hale, Heijer, & Koornneef, 2003, Hopkins, 2004, Rebbit & Erickson, 2016, and Smith, 2016) and too many rules can create unnecessary bureaucracy.

In turn, bureaucracy can undermine the value of rules.

One example of this involved a company who worked on various client sites. In their own yard, the company had a rule that forklift trucks gave way to pedestrians. To help enforce this rule they had a site induction and questionnaire, and one of the questions was a true or false question:

forklifts must give way to pedestrians

For the company site, the answer to this question was "*true*".

This induction/questionnaire had been rolled out to all 15 sites where the company provided services, with an instruction from the health and safety manager that every employee of the company had to complete it, regardless of which site they worked on.

The bureaucracy of this should be immediately apparent – the induction questionnaire was created for one site but used on other sites. The process – having a completed induction questionnaire –

had completely overshadowed the purpose – making sure people were aware of the health and safety hazards on the site where they were working.

This problem was compounded in one case where the client had the opposite rule on their site; pedestrians had to give way to forklifts. Notwithstanding the client requirement, the company maintained the same forklift questionnaire. This meant that workers on that site were saying it was "*true*" that forklifts had to give way to pedestrians, and it was being marked as correct, even though the client requirement was completely the opposite.

Everybody knew what a nonsense this was. All they were interested in was completing the paperwork so people on site would not be hassled by the health and safety manager.

The bureaucracy of this situation – the disconnect between process and purpose – was underscored by the fact the client had approved the induction and questionnaire, promoting an apparent breach of their own rules.

Sometimes, rules can be a problem in their own right, and promote unsafe work practices.

On 6 March 1997 the Roll on/Roll off passenger and freight ferry, Herald of Free Enterprise, sailed from Zeebrugge in Europe, headed for Dover in the United Kingdom. A few minutes into the journey the vessel capsized. 150 passengers and 38 crew members were killed.

While there were a range of factors contributing to the tragedy, the immediate cause of the disaster was described in a subsequent inquiry (Sheen, 1987, p. 8) as follows:

> *The HERALD capsized because she went to sea with her inner and outer bow door open.*

One of the *"rules"*, a standing order, which the inquiry examined was standing order 01.09:

01.09 Ready for Sea

Heads of Departments are to report to the Master immediately they are aware of any deficiency which is likely to cause their departments to be unready for sea in any respect at the due sailing time.

In the absence of any such report the Master will assume, at the due sailing time, that the vehicle is ready for sea in all respects. (Sheen, 1987, p. 12)

As the Court noted, *"[t]hat order was unsatisfactory in many respects"* (Sheen, 1987, p. 12):

Masters came to rely on the absence of any report at the time of sailing as satisfying them that their ship was ready for sea in all respects. That was, of course, a very dangerous assumption. (Sheen, 1987, p. 12).

It is when rules become aligned with paperwork and approval processes, or even when the paperwork and approval processes become more important than the content of the rule, that we really see bureaucracy take hold.

In such cases, we see universally accepted *"good ideas"* crushed under the weight of bureaucracy.

In my experience, it is universally recognised that it is a good idea to stop and think about hazards associated with any work you are about to do. Having thought about the work, you should plan how you are going to do the work to ensure as far as you can, you do it safely. This seems perfectly sensible and helpful – *think about hazards and plan how you are going to do the work.*

Where have we taken this rule?

This rule has spawned a bureaucratic empire, completely out of all proportion to what we are trying to achieve. A mass of paperwork where the process (and key performance indicator) is king, and all memory of purpose is long gone.

This rule is often characterised by documented *"frontline risk assessment procedures"*. These procedures might be documents like a Permit to Work, a Job Hazard Analysis (JHA) or a Take 5.

These processes are typically characterised by a risk assessment and form, where workers must:

- Identify and *document* each step in the work task;

- Identify and *document* each hazard associated with the work step;

- Conduct a risk assessment and assigned a risk rating to each hazard; and

- Identify and *document* each the control measures to manage each work step.

The supervisor of the work must approve the form - apparently *"evidence"* that the form has been *"checked"*.

Sometimes, if the risk ranking is above a certain level (i.e. *"high"*) the form must go to some higher level of management to be approved before the work can start.

Workers often complete this process every time they do the task – even if it is the same task done repeatedly. Workers also must, review and sign the form every day if work is performed over multiple days and update the form if the task changes.

But that is not all.

The frontline risk assessment process will also have a procedure or something similar which describes how it works – a procedure someone had to develop which is reviewed and updated. A procedure people are expected to refer to and apply correctly.

Training also supports the procedure to teach people about the procedure and how to do frontline risk assessment "*properly*". The training is recorded, and records of training are kept in a training database – which again, someone as to manage and maintain. The training database also needs to be monitored so we know when people need retraining.

Of course, the story does not end there.

The frontline risk assessment tools are subject to review. Managers go out into the workplace and review the frontline risk assessment tool to make sure it is done. They also need to "*quiz*" workers about the tool. The management review may also be documented in a checklist, which is kept and stored in a database – which again is managed, maintained and monitored by someone.

Still further review continues.

Many organisations do "*desktop*" checks of frontline risk assessment tools whereby personnel select samples of frontline risk assessment documents and review them to make sure workers have completed them "*properly*". The organisation also captures and records *this* review in the database.

Finally, this activity feeds into a Key Performance Indicator for safety (which is developed, agreed, and reviewed). Many organisations report on the *number of frontline risk assessment tools completed* and reviewed as a key safety metric. This ties up more organisational resources, collecting data, chasing up frontline risk assessment reviews, producing reports etc., etc.

Yet, for all this activity by and large, most organisations have no idea how well frontline workers understand and manage risks. They might know how many frontline risk assessments have been done and reviewed, but they do not know if workers can properly identify the hazards associated with their work, and then plan the work to manage those hazards.

Organisations *assume* a level of understanding and planning based on the amount of activity, but it is a tenuous assumption at best.

Organisational reliance on bureaucracy can lead to a very lax, non-critical approach to managing risk, which becomes an exercise in document completion rather than conversations about an understanding of the risks associated with work.

THE HANDRAIL CONUNDRUM

I n this section, I want to consider rules in the context of bureaucracy, and in particular, removing rules. While removing rules looks attractive in theory, in practice it may not be so simple. Certainly, it is not as simple as just removing rules altogether.

I devoted a chapter on rules in my first book (Smith, 2016). The point I was making at that time was that rules are necessary, but they are just one tool organisations use to help manage health and safety risks in their business. They are not a cure all, and to be effective it must be recognised that rules have limits. More recently, the "*safety differently*" movement has argued that things go "*right*" in organisations because people can adapt their performance to meet the challenges of change, inefficiency and surprise in the workplace. Every day, people get work done and more often than not this requires variation from rules, rather than compliance with them (see for example, Dekker, 2015).

I do not see commentators arguing that we should do away with *all rules*, but there does seem to be a growing call to get rid of "*trivial*" or "*silly*" rules (see for example *Safety Differently: The Movie* https://youtu.be/moh4QN4IAPg). However, getting rid of rules also presents a problem for organisations, and how to balance

40

the relationship between rules and individual initiative, between prescription (telling people what to do) and discretion (letting people decide how to do something) is a real dilemma in organisations.

One example is using a handrail when walking up and down stairs at work.

I had not been introduced to handrail "*rules*" until I started working in the oil and gas industry in 2007 – we did not have such rules in law firms. The simple rule was you always needed to hold the handrail when using the stairs

My immediate, and then long held, reaction to this rule was that it was insulting. It was trivial. An employer did not need to tell me how to use stairs!

In my worldview, my disdain about trivial rules was consistent with the law. For example, in *Transpacific Industrial Solutions Pty Limited v Phelps* [2013] NSWCA 31, a worker was injured moving furniture up a set of stairs. In deciding the case, the Court said:

> *The risk of harm to which the plaintiff succumbed was that of slipping or tripping while ascending stairs. It may be accepted that the risk of slipping or tripping is foreseeable and not insignificant on every occasion on which a person walks up or down a flight of stairs* ([43]).

However, the Court went on to note:

> *The staircase was an ordinary staircase of a type with which everybody is familiar. There is no suggestion that the particular stairs presented any special or unusual risk of tripping or slipping*

and

... The activity of moving furniture is a familiar one... a commonplace activity likely to be encountered, just as frequently, if not more frequently, in the course of ordinary domestic life than in the workplace ([49]).

Referring to an earlier decision, *Seage v State of New South Wales* [2008] NSW CA 328 at [32] – [33], the Court said:

it would be a large step to take to find as a general proposition that employers have an obligation to warn or take other precautions in relation to everyday activities in which employees might incidentally engage in the course of their employment, being activities which if not performed with care might lead to injury. Should employers reasonably be expected to warn employees not to cut themselves when using knives in the staff kitchen? Or not to scold themselves when pouring water which they have boiled for their tea or coffee? Or to be careful when ascending or descending steps? Or not to bump into furniture? ([49]).

In the course of working in and for various organisations over the last 30 years, I have been warned about all of these things. Indeed, in many organisations proactive measures are taken to avoid exposure to these everyday risks, such as banning certain types of knives in the workplace or enforcing a rule to put lids on coffee cups.

However, at another level, these apparently trivial rule makes sense.

We know, for example, people are killed or injured tripping up or falling down stairs – indeed the decision above recognises this. We know this happens. We also know that holding a handrail is a good way to mitigate this risk – it helps prevents people being killed or injured while using stairs.

Gregory Smith

The dilemma seems to be, not that the rule is stupid – the rule makes sense – but rather how we *"bureaucratise"* the rule, how we enforce it, and how we communicate the rule.

If I may, I would like to digress slightly at this point to put this conundrum into a legal context, because legal compliance often drives what we do in the name of health and safety.

In Australia at least, workplace accidents tend to drive three potential legal outcomes. First, there is a risk of being prosecuted under health and safety legislation. Second, organisations and individuals can be sued when people – both workers are members of the public – are injured at a workplace. Third, and probably most problematically, injured workers are entitled to *"no fault"* workers compensation. Almost regardless of how an accident occurs at work an injured worker will receive some form of ongoing financial support and medical assistance with the primary objective of returning to work.

Within this context, when we are talking about workplace rules, like using handrails, it is worth noting a few points.

In my experience, it is very unlikely an organisation will be prosecuted if somebody fell down stairs while not holding a handrail. There is no real history of this type of prosecution in Australia and no examples I can find.

If there was something physically wrong with the stairs, for example they were not built to Australian Standards, or they did not have proper slip resistance, then this could give rise to a prosecution.

However, you cannot defend a prosecution under health and safety legislation using administrative rules – hold the handrail – if the cause of the accident was something physically wrong with the stairs. If something is physically wrong with the stairs the employer must physically fix them.

In the same way, it is very unlikely that an organisation could be sued if somebody falls down stairs unless something is physically wrong with the stairs.

However, if somebody falls down the stairs while at work they will be entitled to workers compensation, almost regardless of the physical state of the stairs or whether the person complied with any rules.

Here we start to see the dilemma develop. Because, if we have a rule, we can be held accountable for it, or at the very least, if there is an injury, our rules and the way we enforce them will be scrutinised.

When looked at in isolation it is very easy to criticise an organisation for not paying enough attention to a rule. But no organisation has unlimited time and resources, and all organisations have many rules – not just in safety.

The dilemma is, with so many rules and limited capacity, we cannot pay attention to everything, and the way we manage rules may even undermine safety in organisations – the Safety Paradox.

We might start with a simple rule – always hold the handrail when using the stairs – but how does the rule translate into practice?

Is it a written rule?

Do we put up posters and signs?

Do we talk about the handrail rule during inductions?

Do we discuss the rule during toolbox talks and prestart meetings?

Is the rule part the written procedure?

Do we investigate instances when people do not use the handrail?

Do we take disciplinary action against people who do not use the handrail?

Is the handrail rule included in refresher and other safety training?

Do we have a handrail or stair use checklist? (And yes, that is a real thing)

Once you begin, the opportunity for bureaucracy and confusion seemed almost endless.

The risk of falling down stairs is not a catastrophic risk, at least not in the sense it might be understood in high hazard industries with the potential for multiple fatalities from a single event, like mining or the oil and gas industry. But it is a risk with potential consequences, and certainly potential cost implications for an employer.

The challenge in this context is not to throw away the rule, rather to understand the rule in our workplace and work out how to communicate the requirement without making the specific rule seem stupid and trivial or detract from the overall health and safety message.

BUREAUCRACY OR COMPLEXITY?

Conversations about improving structural elements of health and safety often frame the conversation as a shift from "*complexity*" to "*simplicity*".

In my view, this is the wrong conversation. Health and safety is complex.

Health and safety is complex because of the sheer number of factors that can align to cause an accident. It is complex because it takes place in a dynamic, ever-changing environment. It is complex because we cannot always foresee the consequences of our actions.

It is, a classic "*wicked problem*" (Rittel & Webber, 1973).

In my view, the conversation ought not be about complexity and simplicity, rather, we should be talking about a shift from bureaucracy to clarity. We should recognise the complexity inherent in managing workplace health and safety hazards, understand the complexity but always strive to provide clarity.

We should recognise *"[c]omplex systems always fail in complex ways"*, (Columbia Accident Investigation Board, 2003, p. 6) and by seeking *"simplicity"* all we might do is hide the complexity and make it harder to understand the potential for failure.

In my experience, the search for simplicity has caused problems and taken us down the path of simple, one size fits all solutions.

One of the most egregious examples of *"ignorant"* simplicity I have seen was a direction in a mining company to its health and safety team that all health and safety procedures had to be less than four pages long.

The problems inherent in this type of approach is obvious. Some processes require detailed instructions and information about how they are implemented and an attempt to mandatorily compress a procedure into a set number of pages threatens to compromise the process. That is not to say we cannot write health and safety processes with greater clarity, and I explore some of these issues later in this book, but a mandatory page limit on a health and safety process seems to me to be the height of bureaucracy gone mad.

Just because we mandate a word limit, does not make the word limit appropriate. Health and safety processes need to be as detailed as they need to be – to be effective. Uncontrolled verbiage and *"unintelligible gobbledygook"* is not helpful, but neither is mandatory word limits which compromises the integrity of the process.

To make matters worse, the solution within the health and safety department to the obvious problem, was to reduce the font size of the text to fit within the mandatory four-page limit. Nothing was done to improve the clarity of information, and if anything, the reduced font size made the documents more difficult and less appealing to read.

Not all examples of *"simplifying safety"* have such obvious problems. Often safety initiatives done in the name of simplifying safety messages seemed good in theory but can have unintended consequences – this is an issue we will explore further when we look at the concept of the Safety Paradox.

One example of how simplification can have unintended consequences, reducing both understanding and clarity are tools such as "*golden rules*". Golden rules usually cover high risk work activities, such as working at heights, working with electricity, or similar activities.

These types of rules have become popular and the basic premise of the rules is to take a relatively complex or detailed safe working instruction, or similar process, and restate it as a basic pictogram with a short statement of requirements.

In one case, an oil and gas company had a golden rule for excavation and ground penetration. The golden rule had a pictogram of an excavator, with a statement to the effect that excavation must not occur unless there was a valid and approved Permit to Work in place.

The rule makes sense in the context of a land-based oil and gas facility, where there was a risk excavation could damage or rupture gas pipelines or electrical cables. The essence of the golden rule was to ensure adequate planning prior to any excavation to find underground services.

The oil and gas company engaged a marine group to provide offshore support services, and one of the conditions of the engagement was the marine group had to follow the company's golden rules. This included training personnel in the golden rules and putting up a poster of the golden rules on the marine vessels.

The difficulty was, the marine group had its own rules for safety that were peculiar to its own, maritime, environment. By insisting on compliance with its golden rules, the oil and gas company compromised safety within the marine group. It added another layer of rules to the way the marine group usually operated and added to the bureaucracy and confusion about how health and safety risks were to be managed.

This problem was compound because the marine group had argued vigorously against having to train its personnel, and display a poster about, ground disturbance and excavation. Although this rule might have made perfect sense in the context of a land-based oil and gas facility, it made no sense on a marine vessel – who was going to be digging a hole?

By dogmatic, almost blind insistence on compliance with its rules – a hallmark of bureaucracy – the oil and gas company not only added unnecessary bureaucracy to safety on the marine vessels, it made safety an object of ridicule. Within the marine group there was no respect for the oil and gas company's attitude toward safety because of their insistence on applying a rule about ground disturbance and excavation to a marine vessel.

A more direct example of how simplicity in the form of golden rules can undermine safety occurred during lifting operations on a mine site.

The mining company had a detailed suite of processes dealing with lifting operations, which included corporate standards, site lifting procedures and lifting plan requirements. The mining company also had a golden rule. The golden rule consisted of a pictogram of a person standing just at the edge of a suspended load, with the statement:

I will never work in the line of fire of a suspended load

During maintenance work on a large vessel, a crane was used to lift sections out of the vessel. One of the sections was dropped during the lift and fell into the vessel.

Two workers were still inside the vessel when the load fell, and it was only a matter of luck that neither of them was seriously injured or killed.

The processes dealing with lifting operations had detailed guidance about setting up exclusion zones when lifting to ensure people were not at risk of being hit by dropped objects. However, an investigation into the incident suggested workers had come to rely on the golden rule for managing the risks associated with lifting operations. Workers had interpreted the golden rule to mean they must not stand *"directly under"* a suspended load. As far as the workers inside the vessel were concerned, they were doing the right thing – they were complying with the golden rule – because they were not *"directly"* under the suspended load.

Cases looking at the issue of bureaucracy in safety management often comment that bureaucracy makes it difficult for workers to understand what they are meant to do, or how to manage hazards associated with their work.

Simplicity is not necessarily an answer to this issue. In fact, simplicity may create the same lack of *"clarity"* bureaucracy does.

Simplicity may offer no greater insight for workers about the hazards associated with the job, the controls to manage the work, why those controls are important or how those controls need to be implemented and applied.

Simplicity in health and safety management has really become a code word for *"easy"*. To make health and safety management *"clear"* for people is not the same thing as making it easy or simple.

Gregory Smith

It is very easy to tell people what to do. It is very easy to just prescribe the way the work must be performed. It takes a lot more effort to provide clarity – to help people understand the health and safety hazards associated with their work and why work needs to be performed in a certain way to make it *"safe"*.

THE SAFETY PARADOX

I t seem to me there are two prevailing mindsets in safety management.

First, more is better. This idea manifests itself in several ways. For example, it seems to be the accepted norm that large safety management plans are better than concise ones. It also seems to be accepted that long, sometimes multi-day inductions are better than a short 20-minute summary of key points.

This *"more is better"* philosophy is also reflected in the idea that we have to keep *"refreshing"* safety or introducing new safety initiatives.

The second mindset seems to assume that all safety initiatives are good. We assume that things done in the name of health and safety will always produce good health and safety outcomes.

I do not think that either of these propositions are inherently correct.

There seems to be a reluctance within the health and safety industry to recognise many health and safety initiatives can undermine workplace safety in practice and doing more *"safety"* just compounds the problem.

Gregory Smith

The Safety Paradox is my way of recognising that health and safety initiatives have the potential to both *improve* and *undermine* safety.

Let me illustrate what I mean using the example of BP Texas City.

On 23 March 2005, the BP Texas City refinery experienced a catastrophic accident. At the time, it was one of the most serious workplace disasters in the United States for nearly two decades, resulting in 15 deaths and more than 170 injuries. (U.S. Chemical Safety and Hazard Investigation Board, 2007).

Subsequent inquiries into the cause of the disaster identified a myriad of technical, cultural and personal issues that interacted on the day. However, investigations also identified that safety management itself may have contributed to the disaster, in the form of *"initiative overload"*:

> *BP's corporate organization has mandated numerous initiatives to its businesses, including its U.S. refineries, during the last several years. Some of these have been directly related to process safety, such as the integrity management standard, process safety minimum expectations, and engineering technical practices. Some have been more focused on personal safety, such as the control of work standard and the driving standard, while others relate to non-safety aspects of HSSE, including environmental and other compliance initiatives. Still other initiatives were driven primarily by commercial considerations, such as the separation for sale to a third party of business assets embedded in sites where BP also conducted refining operations. Each successive initiative has required the refineries to develop plans, conduct analyses, commit resources, and report on progress.*

53

While each initiative has been well intentioned, collectively they have overloaded refinery management and staff. BP's corporate organization has provided the refineries with little guidance on how to prioritize these many initiatives, and the refineries do not receive additional funding to implement each initiative. As a result, senior refinery managers used phrases such as "initiative overload," "incoming," and "unfunded mandates" to describe what they perceived as an avalanche of programs and endeavors that compete for funding and attention. The ripple effects are then felt throughout the refinery. Many of the hourly workers interviewed at all of the refineries complained that the large number of initiatives and related paperwork contributed to a heavy workload and prevented the workforce from being as focused on safety and operations as they would like. They also reported that the repeated launch of each successive initiative made it increasingly difficult for the workforce to take any of these initiatives seriously; many interviewees described this as the "flavor of the month" phenomenon. This situation has existed for a number of years. As a 2004 third-party consultant report on Toledo observed:

Safety policies, programs and procedures, according to many have value, but are reaching a saturation point. Some add that there are too many safety programs that "miss the mark" and those that are effective are only occasionally seen through to completion (my emphasis added) (Baker, et al., 2007, p. 86).

Paradoxically, in this case, the number of safety initiatives may have undermined BP's attempts to achieve a safe workplace:

This "initiative overload" may have undermined process safety performance at the U.S. refineries (Baker, et al., 2007, p. xii).

54

Gregory Smith

Another example is the potential for health and safety management to adversely impact the mental health and well-being of workers.

Most health and safety legislation in Australia expressly includes psychological health within its remit, or psychological health is acknowledged to fall under health and safety legislation. For example, the Western Australian Department of Mines and Petroleum has acknowledged that they regard *"health"* as including *"psychological"* health, even though the State's mining legislation does not expressly refer to psychological health (Education and Health Standing Committee, 2015, pp. 42, 43).

At the same time, what is emerging, at least to my mind, is the extent to which our policy, procedure and policing approach to safety and health, far from alleviating psychological harm in the workplace, might be contributing to it.

Safety management might be part of the problem.

In an inquiry into the possible impact of fly in/fly out work on *"mental health"* the Australian Medical Association identified that the way health and safety is managed can contribute to a *"distinct sense of entrapment"* (Education and Health Standing Committee, 2014, p. 43):

> The AMA also expressed its concerns about this issue, noting that *"[o]nerous rules, safety procedures and focus on achievement of production levels have been shown to create a distinct sense of entrapment in FIFO workers.*

The inquiry drew, in some measure, on an earlier report (Sellenger Centre for Research in Law, Justice and Social Change, 2013), (**Lifeline Report**) which also noted the adverse impact of safety and health management on psychological well-being. For example, *"[a]dhering to on-site safety rules"* was identified as a *workplace stress* (Sellenger Centre for Research in Law, Justice and Social Change, 2013, p. 77).

Interestingly, the Lifeline Report noted a sense of *"intimidation"* brought on by the number of rules and regulations associated with work on a mine, and:

> *This sense of intimidation was further mirrored in the outcomes of mining safety regulations which in theory were designed to care for workers but in practice led to inflexible regulation over genuine safety concerns* (Sellenger Centre for Research in Law, Justice and Social Change, 2013, p. 81).

Examples from the Lifeline Report include:

> *... a participant recalled a situation in which a worker handling heavy loads required an adhesive bandage but was unable to ask someone to get them for him because he had to fill out an accident report first (which he was unable to do mid-job); hence he had to carry on working without attending to his cuts. Alternatively, another example of the application of safety rules in an inflexible manner was illustrated when a group of workers were reprimanded for not wearing safety glasses on a 40 degree day even though they could not see from them due to excessive sweating. Hence, safety rules themselves were accepted as a necessary part of work but their implementation in an inflexible uniform manner created stress as workers felt their impact hindered their ability to conduct basic work tasks safely and/or without attracting rebuke. Hence, site rules and regulations could translate into arbitrary and punitive forms of punishment, which undermined participants' ability to fulfil jobs to their satisfaction and left them feeling insecure with their positions.* (Sellenger Centre for Research in Law, Justice and Social Change, 2013, p. 81)

Gregory Smith

It seems, then, that we need to think beyond our own perceptions of what might contribute to workplace stress and understand the impact that our efforts to manage health and safety might actually be having. Again, as the Lifeline Report noted:

> *... although past research has shown that site conditions and cultures, such as isolation and excessive drinking are problematic, this research shows that the regimented nature of working and living on-site also takes a toll on mental health and wellbeing. From the responses of many participants, it was apparent that **following site safety rules** (either under pressure of internal monitoring or in the perceived absence of adequate safety precautions by co-workers and supervisors) **was a significant stressor**. Participants felt unable to apply self-perceived common-sense judgments and also reported **feeling vulnerable to intensive scrutinising, intimidation and threats of job loss**.* (my emphasis added) (Sellenger Centre for Research in Law, Justice and Social Change, 2013, p. 81).

Paradoxically, in this case, efforts to manage health and safety risks through *"traditional"* safety management may be contributing to harm in mental health.

THE ILLUSION OF SAFETY

While bureaucratic health and safety management systems can often undermine the efforts of an organisation to achieve a safe workplace, an additional and compounding problem with bureaucracy in safety is it often "*masks*" the true state of health and safety performance.

Bureaucratic health and safety management often contributes to the "*illusion of safety*" (Hollnagel, Woods, & Leveson, 2008).

The illusion of safety refers to the "*gap*" between safety as it is "*imagined*" and work as it is actually performed.

At its most basic, the illusion of safety refers to an unfounded and unsubstantiated belief that policies, procedures, processes and other documentation coupled with lots of "*activity*" in the name of health and safety, means that health and safety risks are being effectively managed. History would suggest this is not the case.

Here, we can see the relationship between the Safety Paradox and the illusion of safety. For example, from a senior leadership position in an organisation you might perceive numerous and ongoing safety initiatives as an indication health and safety was being managed well, whereas the reality on the ground may well be safety processes are being ignored because of *"initiative overload"*.

As you read this book, you will find many examples of cases where an organisation relied on documented systems to manage health and safety risks, but those systems have amounted to little more than window dressing – workers going through a mechanistic tick and flick process to discharge the bureaucratic requirement without any evidence that the health and safety risk is actually controlled.

An example of such a case is the New South Wales Supreme Court decision, *Attorney General of New South Wales v Tho Services Limited (in liquidation) (ACN 000 263 678)* [2016] NSWCCA 221.

This case is just one in a long histpry of decisions highlighting the disconnect between safety management systems as they are documented, and what occurs in practice.

In March 2013, a 15-year-old student was doing work experience at Tho Services Limited. The workshop manager gave the student a visitor's induction and the leading hand supervised him during the day.

The student performed welding tasks during the day and was provided with personal safety equipment, including a welding mask. The mask used an adjustable visor that had to be lowered manually to protect a welder's eyes from the damaging effects of ultra violet light when welding. Despite the provision of this equipment, and the ostensible supervision, the student performed welding work throughout the day without lowering his protective visor. As a result, he sustained significant, permanent damage to his eyes. He was left with a 75 percent bilateral visual incapacity.

Tho pleaded guilty to the charge, which was dismissed by the Magistrate at first instance with no penalty being imposed. The Magistrate stated:

In the present circumstances I do not find it necessary to denounce the conduct of the offender. I am satisfied from all of the material that the offender took all reasonable institutional measures to ensure compliance with the Act. [5]

The "*institutional measures*" included:

- An induction and induction document which the student had to read and sign;

- A "*Golden Rules to LIVE by*" document which the student had to read and sign;

- A "*Job Safety & Environmental Analysis*" which the leading hand discussed with the student; and

- Various training programs on health and safety for supervisors.

The student had some experience welding previously at school, but on those occasions, had used an "*automatic element*", where the visor automatically darkened to adapt to the light emitted by welding. The student said that he had never seen a welding helmet with a flip down visor previously and had never used such a helmet.

When the student started welding, at about 9am, the leading hand saw him "*welding correctly*", as he had been shown, including with the visor on his helmet down.

At about 2:20 pm an afternoon shift worker saw the student welding with the visor up and told him to stop. The shift worker and afternoon shift leading hand spoke to the student and asked him why he was welding visor up, and he told them he did not know he had to wear the visor down and had been welding with the visor in the up position all day.

The finding by the Magistrate at first instance was appealed, on the basis that dismissing the charge without penalty was manifestly inadequate. On appeal, the Supreme Court agreed and imposed a penalty of $240,000.

The Court made several observations about the management of the student, in particular:

- He was not told the visor must be down;

- He was not told his eyes may be damaged if he did not use the visor; and

- He was welding on and off throughout the day, unsupervised, with his visor up.

The Court said:

[The Supervisor] did not provide [the Student] with any information, instruction or demonstration in how to use the welding helmets which were provided. Nor did he inform him of the risk of damaging his eyes if he failed to use the helmet's visor correctly. [36]

In upholding the appeal, the Supreme Court said that dismissing the charge without penalty was manifestly inadequate:

The breach was flagrant. It resulted from an egregious and systemic failure to supervise a young and vulnerable person. [60]

The Court drew a distinction between measures to ensure compliance with the Act and practically ensuring health and safety:

There is in my view an irreconcilable tension between his Honour's finding that the respondent took all reasonable institutional measures to ensure compliance with the Act on the one hand and the fact that notwithstanding those measures a work experience student was severely injured on the other hand. With respect to his Honour, he has approached the matter somewhat mechanistically, eliding the respondent's perfunctory performance of its statutory obligations with the absence of responsibility for what occurred. It is clear that at some point during the day in question, Mr Thomas was welding in full view of the respondent's employees without a protective visor in place. A more obvious failure of safety protocols is difficult to imagine. It therefore lies ill in the mouth of the respondent in those circumstances to say that the necessary induction process had been carried out or that the respondent's supervising employees had been properly trained. **Such an approach would unacceptably see the elevation of form over substance to the possible detriment of practical safety implementation** *and would in effect authorise or excuse the less than optimal discharge of the obligation to take reasonable and proper care for the safety of employees and, in the present case, work experience students.* (my emphasis added) [64].

This criticism of *"form over substance"*, in many ways strikes at the heart of the modern health and safety industry.

Documented safety processes are important. They provide guidance on how safety is managed and evidence that an organisation is meeting its obligations. However, where an accident reveals long-term, systemic non-compliance with obvious safety expectations, documented safety processes do not provide a defence, often they do not provide mitigation, and in cases such as this they are an aggravating circumstance. As the Court noted:

> The vast range of induction and supervising protocols adopted by the respondent or in force at its premises serves not to relieve the respondent of its responsibility for safety but on the contrary **powerfully reinforces the extent to which the respondent failed to put them into practical effect**. (my emphasis added) [90].

In this and other cases throughout the book, it may be arguable whether the safety management processes undermined safety performance, but it does seem the organisations involved placed reliance on the processes, assuming because the processes were in place, safety was being managed. In fact, it appears bureaucratic layering of safety processes disguised the true state of safety management, or at least prevented the organisation from understanding the true state of safety management.

I will examine other examples of bureaucracy in health and safety management, and how bureaucracy can act to hide the true state of safety management in an organisation later in this book. But for now, I would like to use one example to illustrate the role bureaucracy can play perpetuating the illusion of safety or hiding the "*gap*" between work as it is imagined and work as it is performed, in this case in the context of aircraft maintenance:

> Commercial aircraft line maintenance is emblematic: a job perception gap exists where supervisors are convinced that safety and success result from mechanics following procedures – **a sign off means that applicable procedures were followed**. But mechanics may encounter problems for which the right tools or parts are not at hand; the aircraft may be part far away from base. Or there may be too little time: aircraft with a considerable number of problems may have to be turned around for the next flight within half an hour.

*Mechanics, consequently, see success as the result of their evolved skills at adapting, inventing, compromising, and improvising in the face of local pressure and challenges on the line – **a sign off means the job was accomplished in spite of resource limitations, organisational dilemmas, and pressures chronicling** (my emphasis added) (Dekker S. , 2008, p. 86).*

In this case it seems process has become disconnected from purpose at every level of the organisation, both the workforce and management. Workers are content to play along with the bureaucratic process, notwithstanding that it does not honestly represent what they are doing. Management are prepared to accept the bureaucratic process without challenge and are willing to assume the process represents their idealised belief about what is occurring in practice.

In neither case does the acceptance of the bureaucratic process positively contribute to a better safety outcome.

Gregory Smith

ONE–OFF DEPARTURE OR SYSTEMIC FAILURE

In considering bureaucracy in the context of safety management we should recognise that not every poorly completed document or missed inspection means the system has failed or has become too bureaucratic. We must recognise people are fallible and they will make mistakes. At times, it is true, people will deliberately shortcut or bypass safety processes. Again, neither of these scenarios means the system is inherently or overly bureaucratic.

However, we also need to recognise that failure in process, while it might simply be a *"one-off departure"* in an otherwise effective (not bureaucratic) system, it might also be evidence of systemic failure.

In *Safe Work NSW v Wollongong Glass P/L* [2016] NSWDC 58, a worker was killed when they were crushed under the weight of several glass panels. In considering the case, the Court implicitly considered the distinction between a one-off departure and a systemic failure, and identified that a one-off departure from an otherwise effective system was legally defensible:

> *Where an employer is found to have laid down a safe and proper practice and there is no evidence that the*

65

employer failed to use due diligence to see that the practice is observed, then a casual failure by inferior employees, even if of a supervisory rank, to observe that practice on a particular occasion will not render the employer criminally liable for a failure to ensure safety: Collins v State Rail Authority of New South Wales (1986) 5 NSWLR 209 at 215E. ([32])

This position, *"proper"* practices and *"due diligence"*, particularly due diligence, is often absent when we look at workplace accidents.

On 6 July 1988, 167 people died following a catastrophic fire at the offshore oil producing platform, Piper Alpha. The subsequent inquiry into the disaster (Cullen, 1990), identify the failure of the Permit to Work system as a critical (if not the) causal factor in the disaster. However, the failure of the Permit to Work system was not a one-off departure from an otherwise effective process:

*Earlier in this report I reached the conclusion that a failure in the [Permit to Work (**PTW**)] system had occurred on the evening of the disaster and that if this had not occurred Mr Vernon would not have attempted to restart condensate injection pump A and thus unwittingly caused a leap of condensate... The evidence which I considered in Chapter 11 showed that this failure was not an isolated mistake but that in a number of respects the PTW system was **being operated routinely in a casual and unsafe manner**. That evidence along with the evidence to which I have referred to earlier in this chapter shows, in my view, the operation of the PTW system was not being adequately monitored or audited. These were failures for which management were responsible. If there had been adequate monitoring and auditing it is likely that these deficiencies in the PTW system would have been corrected.* (my emphasis added) (Cullen, 1990, p. 231)

66

As we will see in many examples cited in this book, departures from documented ways of working – the system as it is imagined – are seldom one-off departures. Departures from documented ways of working are typically systemic failures brought about by change over time to the point they become *"normalised"*, the accepted way of working.

In *Fry v Keating* [2013] WASC 109, A worker was killed during lifting operations when a load being lifted by a crane slipped and fell. There was a *"proper"* process for doing the work, a method of lifting which the Court described as Method 1, but over time the workers had developed their own way of doing the work, Method 2.

The use of Method 2 on the day the incident was not a one-off departure. The use of Method 2 represented a systemic failure. The extent to which Method 2 had been normalised was underscored by the finding:

> *Five employees, who were recent employees prior to the accident, believed, based in part on instructions from more senior doggers/riggers, that Method 2 was the method to be used in moving L68 Packs at the workplace ... ([19])*

In my experience systemic failure is both a product of and is reinforced by, bureaucracy in safety management.

Systemic failure is a product of bureaucracy because bureaucratic processes invite, if not leave the workers with no choice but to, work around process. Safety processes are often imposed *"on high"* from safety departments and workers have little understanding of why they are necessary. This is magnified when the documented processes are not consistent with the way work needs to be performed. This lack of explanation combined with a lack of application often means workers:

- Do not see the need to comply the process; or

- Have no choice but to work around the process; and

- Do not feel the need to discuss the shortcomings in the process or are actively discouraged from doing so.

Bureaucracy reinforces systemic failure because our systems of monitoring and reporting are not attuned to systemic failure and are more interested in understanding whether activity has been completed, rather than whether risks are being managed.

PART 2
BUREAUCRACY IN ACTION

GENERAL

I t is a common and recurrent theme that health and safety systems are too difficult for people to use. They do not add value to the day-to-day management of health and safety.

This complaint is common in discussions with all levels of an organisation, managers, supervisors and workers alike. But it is more than just a workforce complaint, and it is something borne out in almost every prosecution and inquiry I have reviewed. Somehow, the process of health and safety management creates systems that become completely disconnected from the purpose for which they are designed – creating safe workplaces – and safety management systems become an *industry* or *enterprise* in their own right. Indeed, the Royal Commission into the Esso Longford Gas Plant explosion said as much, in quite direct terms (Dawson & Brooks, 1999).

Esso Australia Resources Ltd ran several gas plants in south-eastern Victoria, Australia to process gas from wells in Bass Strait. On Friday, 25 September 1998, a vessel in Gas Plant 1 fractured, releasing hydrocarbon vapours and liquid. Explosions and a fire followed. Two Esso employees were killed, and eight others were injured. Supplies of natural gas to customers in Victoria were cut off.

Gregory Smith

In response to the disaster, the Victorian government established a Royal Commission (Dawson & Brooks, 1999) to report on the causes of the explosion and fire, which like so many of the other cases we have looked at, was critical of documented safety management processes.

> *Evidence was given that [Operations Integrity Management System (**OIMS**)], was a world-class system and complied with world best practice. Whilst this may be true of the expectations and guidelines upon which the system was based, the same cannot be said of the operation of the system in practice. Even the best management system is defective if it is not effectively implemented. The system must be capable of being understood by those expected to implement it.*
>
> *Esso's OIMS, together with all the supporting manuals, comprised a complex management system. It was repetitive, circular, and contained unnecessary cross referencing. Much of its language was impenetrable. These characteristics make the system difficult to comprehend both by management and by operations personnel.*
>
> *The Commission gained the distinct impression that there was a tendency for the administration of OIMS to take on a life of its own, divorced from operations in the field. Indeed, it seemed that in some respects,* ***concentration upon the development and maintenance of the system diverted attention from what was actually happening in the practical functioning of the plants at Longford.***
>
> ...
>
> *Reliance placed by Esso on its OIMS for the safe operation of the plant was misplaced* (my emphasis added) (Dawson & Brooks, 1999, p. 200).

71

This example shows how safety can become an end in itself, disconnected from purpose, or to adopt the language of the Royal Commission, "*divorced from operations in the field*".

Esso is also another example of the Safety Paradox. On its face, developing safety management systems *should* benefit safety. Indeed, this seems to be the logic behind the proliferation in safety system accreditation. However, the development and maintenance of these systems can become the goal; not only are they disconnected from purpose, they positively undermine safety by "*diverting attention*" from what is happening in the field.

Later in this book I will go further and argue this type of bureaucracy, which focuses on systems as the goal, not only diverts attention from the true state of safety in organisations, it often creates a positively misleading picture about what is going on.

The Esso Royal Commission is just one example in a long history of public inquiries which criticise the nature of safety management systems. Bureaucratic, documented safety management systems have become one of the key characteristics of safety management over the last 20 or 30 years. The systems are characterised by poorly written procedures, multiple levels and layers of forms, and apparently never-ending checklists for all sorts of activities.

In my experience, bureaucracy in safety management creates a range of problems, but at its core bureaucracy does two things. First, it impacts on the workers. Bureaucracy can make it difficult for workers to understand what they should be doing to manage health and safety risks associated with their work. Bureaucracy can often "*distract*" workers – they end up spending more time doing paperwork and following process than thinking about risk. Bureaucracy can also disengage workers from an organisation's safety management. Bureaucracy can make workers cynical about safety management, seeing it as a process to protect the organisation and its management rather than protect them.

Second, and equally important, bureaucracy can obscure safety management. Bureaucracy makes it very difficult for management to understand whether health and safety risks are being effectively managed in their organisation. Bureaucracy often substitute activity for achievement so senior managers see lots of "*activity*" being done in the name of safety and health as evidenced by forms, records, lead indicators, charts and so on and mistakenly equate this activity with effective safety management.

Almost every major accident inquiry on the planet for the last 30 years, since at least Chernobyl in 1986 (International Nuclear Safety Advisory Group, 1986; International Nuclear Safety Advisory Group, 1992), has found the documented safety management systems in place to manage health and safety, and other risks were not helpful. In many cases, they were too bureaucratic for the people who had to implement them to understand.

We have already seen an example of how bureaucratic safety management processes – initiative overload – can reduce the understanding of health and safety in a workplace, in the BP Texas City example (Baker, et al., 2007, U.S. Chemical Safety and Hazard Investigation Board, 2007). However, history is littered with similar examples, and I have discussed several of these examples below.

Chernobyl

On April 26, 1986 a catastrophic Accident occurred at the Chernobyl nuclear power plant in Ukraine. 28 reactor staff and emergency workers died from radiation and thermal burns within four months of the accident, and officials believe the accident was also responsible for nearly 7000 cases of thyroid cancer in individuals who are under 18 years of age at the time of the accident. Post-accident enquiries found a range of flawed design issues and human error contributed to the accident (See for example, International Nuclear Safety Advisory Group, 1986). While human error clearly played a role, subsequent analysis also identified issues with the quality of safety management processes:

> *The weight given in INSAG-1 in 1986 to the Soviet view presented at the Vienna meeting, which laid blame almost entirely on actions of the operating staff, is hereby lessened. Certain actions by operators were identified in INSAG-1 as violations of rules were in fact not violations. Yet INSAG remains of the opinion that critical actions by operators were most ill judged. As pointed out in INSAG-1, the human factor has still to be considered as a major element in causing the accident.* ***The poor quality of operating procedures and instructions, and their conflicting character, put a heavy burden on the operating crew, including the Chief Engineer*** (my emphasis added) (International Nuclear Safety Advisory Group, 1992, p. 24).

Pike River

On 19 November 2010 a catastrophic explosion occurred at the Pike River underground coal mine in New Zealand. 29 men died in the disaster.

The New Zealand government commissioned a Royal Commission (Panckhurst, Bell, & Henry, 2012) to enquire into the disaster, and just like the other cases we have started to explore, the Royal Commission examined the documented safety management systems in place at Pike River, and found them wanting:

Gregory Smith

> *By November 2010 there were over 398 documents in the electronic system. Of these 227 were in draft as they were not signed off by two managers, although they were still used in the meantime.* **The number, and length, of the documents posed a challenge to the credibility of the system** *(my emphasis added)* (Panckhurst, Bell, & Henry, 2012, p. 73).

Montara

On 21 August 2009, the H1 Well at the Montara Well Head Platform *"kicked"* shooting a column of oil, fluid and gas from the top of the well, through the hatch on the top deck of the Well Head Platform, hitting the underside of the West Atlas drilling rig and cascading into the sea. For just over 10 weeks, oil and gas flowed into the Timor Sea, approximately 250 kilometres off the northwest coast of Australia. At various times, the spill was likely to have affected an area as large as 90,000 square kilometres.

This event was Australia's third largest oil spill by volume, and the worst of its kind in Australia's offshore petroleum industry history.

In response to the event, the Australian government started an inquiry into the causes of the disaster (Borthwick, 2010). Along with several technical findings, the Montara Commission was critical of the relevant company's systems and procedures:

> *In essence, the way that PTTEPAA operated the Montara Oilfield did not come within a 'bulls roar' of sensible oilfield practice. The Blowout was not a reflection of one unfortunate incident, or of bad luck. What happened with the H1 Well was an accident waiting to happen; the company's systems and processes were so deficient and its key personnel so lacking in basic competence, that the*

Blowout can properly be said to have been an event waiting to occur. Indeed, during the course of its public hearing, the Inquiry discovered that not one of the five Montara wells currently complies with the company's Well Construction Standards. Indeed, so poor has PTTEPAA's performance been on the Montara Oilfield, the Inquiry considers it is imperative that remedial action be instituted (Borthwick, 2010, p. 11).

As with the cases we have already looked at, the Montara Commission was also critical of the lack of clarity of documented processes:

*Moreover, the SIMOPS documents were **replete with delphic 'motherhood' statements,** such as the following:*

Safety management in the field is primarily the responsibility of the Vessel Masters/Superintendents, FPSO OIM, Rig OIM and WHP Person In Charge (PIC). The prioritisation of all activities in the Montara field is the responsibility of the PTTEPAA Project Manager. However, control of the individual activities during the field development remains with the relevant supervisors.

...

All parties in the Montara field development shall have clear structuring of HSE interfaces to ensure that there is no confusion as to: approval authority; roles and responsibilities of personnel; organisational structures, management of HSE; operating procedures; reporting structures; and SIMOPS.

General statements of this kind are well and good, but they do little to guard against the sort of marginalising of the OIM's role as occurred at the Montara Oilfield in relation to well control (my emphasis added) (Borthwick, 2010, pp. 135 - 136).

Concerns about documented safety management systems are not limited to significant, major accident events, nor to safety management systems overall.

Systemic bureaucracy, bureaucracy which characterises the overall safety management system, not just part of it, is clear in most workplace accidents, and at every level and every process.

Coroner's Inquest – Cole

In 2009, a worker was killed when a load fell off a truck. A later inquiry by the Queensland coroner (Inquest into the death of Cameron Brandt Cole, 2015) found, amongst many factors:

> *The identification, elimination or minimisation of risks through risk management processes may lead to the production of a suite of documentation that will pass audit requirements. However, the evidence that this inquest suggests that **workers in the field may find such documents hard to comprehend and of limited relevance to their daily activities** (my emphasis added) (Inquest into the death of Cameron Brandt Cole, 2015, p. 24).*

Final Thoughts

Many of our documented processes have become meaningless in practice.

Far from providing, or ensuring safe workplaces, complex and bureaucratic safety management systems are disengaging our workforce and diminishing the standing of health and safety in our organisations.

For many workers, more than being ineffective, safety management is seen as a tool to protect managers, not workers, and to blame workers when something goes wrong.

In his excellent article looking at risk awareness programs, Australian researcher David Borys (Borys, 2009) notes:

> *Workers did not value the program, in particular the paperwork, viewing the paperwork as a means for managers to protect themselves from any threat of prosecution. A typical worker response was: I can't see anybody who's doing it other than to do the paperwork or more bluntly: it's all arse-covering at the end of the day. Ironically, the collection of the paperwork by managers gave them a sense of security that workers were working safely; a sense that is well summed up by the following comment: I feel comfortable that they have a process that enables them to have a safe worksite* (Borys, 2009, p. 6).

Moreover, safety bureaucracy has come to define "*safety*" in organisations. Bureaucracy defines the relationship between the safety function and the organisation.

> *It seems clear, a significant part of the role of a health and safety person in an organisation is taken up with bureaucracy: writing policies and procedures, documenting and auditing safety processes, inspections, regulatory compliance, reports and so on. Safety becomes the "compliance police" continually enforcing negative messages in the organisation such as disciplinary action, non-compliance, incidents, deviations, all which leaves the workforce defensive and in many cases hostile towards the safety department* (see for example Provan, Dekker, & Rae, 2017).

Gregory Smith

The common misconception is reliance on process is necessary to manage legal risk. Indeed, it seems that over the years the role of health and safety industry has been to transition from the management of health and safety risk to the management of legal obligations and legal liability.

The reality is bureaucracy is not necessary to manage legal risk, and often increases legal risk. For most organisations, the biggest source of legal liability following a workplace accident is the level of non-compliance with their own documented procedures.

As many of the examples above illustrate, the bureaucracy in an organisation's safety management is often cause for judicial criticism not legal protection. This is certainly common in health and safety prosecutions in Australia.

In September 2017, a company was convicted and fined $1.13 million after a worker was killed in a forklift incident. The case identified the company had two written procedures for working safely around forklifts. The procedure for the separation of the forklift from workers was set out in a safety diagram. However, the employees were not aware of these procedures, had not been provided with information, instruction or training about the procedures for working around forklifts and the forklift driver had not been trained on the safety procedures (Poultry contractor fined $1.13m over forklift tragedy, 2017).

Unfortunately, this disconnect between documented process and workers is not uncommon. I cannot help but ask, what was the point of developing these "*written work procedures*" if not to inform the workers about how to do the work safely? And if the workers were not given the information they needed to work safely, what was the point of the exercise?

It is very tempting to suspect the purpose of developing the work procedures had nothing to do with safety at any real level, rather if fulfilled some bureaucratic requirement. Equally, however, if we could break the bureaucratic mindset which has infected health and safety and focus on purpose – how do we keep people safe – we might find that moving away from an overreliance on documented process is not only a better way to keep people safe, it is a better way to manage our health and safety obligations.

A 2015 decision, *Inspector McCarthy (nee Shaw) v Siva & Jeya Pty Ltd* [2015] NSDC 15, considered the use and appropriateness of written work instructions.

The case involved serious injuries to a restaurant worker when she was burned refilling burner pots using methylated spirits. The burner pots we used to heat food in bains-marie.

One of the allegations against the employer was that they did not provide the employee with a written safe work method or written directions for the task of refilling burner pots. The reference to "*safe work method*" was not a reference to Safe Work Method Statements required under some health and safety legislation for some high-risk activities. It was just a reference to a safe way to do the work.

Although the employer was convicted for breaches of health and safety legislation on several points, on the specific issue of a written safe work method, the Court said:

> *I do not think that the case for providing her with a written safe work method is made good. The written documentation for an immigrant such as Anisha may be difficult to comprehend and follow and may not necessarily be effective. A spoken direction is more likely to be effective.* [51]

Gregory Smith

One of the risks when safety management systems become overly bureaucratic is people do not think critically about risks and how they are going to control them. It is far too easy to simply reach for documented processes to meet a perceived safety requirement, when documentation may not be the best way to manage the risk, or indeed could even make the workplace less safe.

As I have already said, I am not trying to argue there is no place for rules and documentation in health and safety management, but like anything else in life, they should be taken in moderation. Organisations require ongoing vigilance to understand if the pendulum has swung too far – are the number and content of our rules and documents having a negative impact on safety?

A characteristic of highly bureaucratic management systems is the triumph of form over substance. Compliance with the system appears to become the main objective of management, rather than understanding and demonstrating that the system is achieving the purpose for which it was designed.

It is an unsettling fact, but true nevertheless, that often workers cannot explain the reason why they must do things for safety and health – how health and safety *"activities"* make things safer – they just must do them.

They do not understand the *"purpose"* of their safety activities.

One of the interesting things to note about safety management systems across many organisations is how consistent they are. In other words, many organisations manage health and safety in the same way, using the same forms, completing the same checklists and often plagiarising each other's procedures. It would be difficult to count the number of times I have reviewed procedures after an incident, that refer to other organisations - not their own.

Something else that seems common across safety management systems, is that many of the bureaucratic requirements are blamed on *"legal obligations"*. Certain forms must be completed, checklists must be done because they are *"legal requirements"*. Often, however, no such legal requirement exists.

The nature of safety management, as illustrated by these examples, can create an impression of *"intellectual laziness"*. Safety departments are just doing activities in the name of health and safety because that is what everybody else does, or that is what we have always done and there is no obvious justification, reason or benefit for why these things are being done. Whenever somebody tries to challenge processes in safety management systems, they are fobbed off by being told it is a legal requirement.

There seems to be a general unwillingness to challenge the way that health and safety is managed, to question the value of our processes and to de-clutter and simplify the health and safety expectations imposed on our workforce.

I cannot say with absolute certainty, but my overwhelming sense is that organisations do not want to let go of high process bureaucratic systems because of the misplaced confidence those systems will protect them if there are legal proceedings.

It should be clear from the examples in this book, this is not the case.

Gregory Smith

WHO ARE YOU WRITING FOR?

T he observation in the Esso Royal Commission (Dawson & Brooks, 1999) about systems becoming divorced from operations in the field, and the consistent repetition of this theme over the decades, should have organisations in a constant state of vigilance about the content and quality of their documented processes. Sadly, however, it is difficult to make a case that anything has changed.

I studied law from 1986 until 1990. I practised as an article clerk from 1990 until 1992, when I was admitted to legal practice. So now, by 2018, I have been learning about the law and legal practice for 32 years. In all that time, one of the most consistent messages I have always heard, from teachers, mentors, clients and other lawyers is not to try and write how you think lawyers write.

Safety procedures are not legislation. They are not contractual documents. They are not submissions to the High Court. They are documents that are designed to be used *by your workforce* to keep them safe.

Let me give you an example of some of the problems we have to manage. A client asked me to review a Working at Heights procedure document that had been written for them by a consultant. In my experience, the language of the document was extraordinary. It was convoluted nonsense that left me completely baffled. A typical sentence was:

Working at Height consideration should be given to the possibility and feasibility of carrying out the work by alternate methods to eliminate or minimise the need to work at height.

As far as anybody could tell, all the author was trying to say was "*work on the ground when you can*".

This went on for 15 pages and workers were expected to sign off that they had read and understood the process.

It seems to me, many of our complexity and bureaucracy issues in safety management would disappear if we simply applied some basic, plain English writing.

One of the biggest concerns with safety management documents I see post-accident, is the use of "*references*". These are typically Standards, Codes of Practice or similar guidance material.

Again, by way of example, I can refer to the Working at Height procedure discussed earlier, which contained the following:

Comply with [Australian and New Zealand Standards (AS/NZS)]4576 Guidelines for Scaffolding, BSEN 1263.2.2002 Safety Nets

And

Comply with AS/NZS 4389

And

84

Anchor loading requirements for use with static lines (e.g.: horizontal cables) are usually substantially higher than those used for personal fall arrest equipment. Hence all anchorage points for static lines must be approved in accordance AS.1891.2.

And

There must be a system for ensuring that permanent anchorage points and permanent horizontal life lines are regularly inspected, tested and approved in accordance with AS/NZS 1891.4 by a competent person

The organisation did not have copies of any of the referenced Standards and had no intention of buying them. None of the workers who were supposed to follow the requirements of the Standards had heard of them, much less read them and understood them.

There was no explanation in the Working at Height procedure about what somebody might do to *"Comply with AS/NZS 4389"*. There was no plan to develop or provide training about what any of the Standards meant or how workers might comply with them.

All the references to the Standards had achieved was to make the Working at Height procedure more complicated than it needed to be, inaccessible to the workforce, and unhelpful to manage working at height risk. At the same time, the Working at Height procedure had increased the legal risk to the organisation because it had spelt out a whole range of *"things"* the organisation was going to do to manage the health and safety risks associated with working at height – but those things would never be done because nobody knew what they were.

The truth is, many of our documented safety processes look like this and have been signed off by several layers of management as part of the approval process. The fact that documents like this can persist in our organisations gives rise to a number of questions. Do people actually believe these documents make sense? Do they genuinely think workers understand and are influenced by them? How can managers think work is being performed as described in the documents?

Has anybody actually read these documents?

Do we care about safety, or just the appearance of safety?

Gregory Smith

AUDITS AND ACCREDITATION

One of the most significant subsets of the health and safety industry is the audit and accreditation industry. I cannot recount how many times I have spoken to clients desperate to achieve some level of industry accreditation as part of a contract requirement. These organisations had no real intention of using the accredited system as a means to manage risk. There was no recognition of the effort it would take to embed an accredited system in their organisation, to train workers on the system or to communicate the requirements. Accreditation was a certificate on the wall and a folder full of process that could be rolled out to win work, during contract reviews and during audits.

In many ways, audit and accreditation have become the window dressing of health and safety management – a shiny exterior, with no need to look deeper.

The Cole Inquiry (Inquest into the death of Cameron Brandt Cole, 2015, p. 24) observed:

> *The identification, elimination or minimisation of risks through risk management processes may lead to the **production of a suite of documentation that will pass audit requirements**.*(my emphasis added)

One of the interesting issues to emerge in relation to audits and accreditation is the shift from those processes being used to confirm the efficacy of safety systems, to safety systems being developed to meet the requirements of audits and accreditation – irrespective of the impact on safety. It has been noted:

> *Far from being passive, audit actively constructs the context in which it operates.* (Michael, 1996, p. 7)

This certainly seems to have been the experience of health and safety.

If the case studies in this book so far tell us anything, it should be that compliance with audit requirements (Paper Safe) do not mean, or should not be equated with, safe work practices. There are numerous cases of serious workplace accidents where inquiries have gone out of their way to note the disconnect between outstanding audit results and workplace practices.

Comcare v John Holland Pty Ltd [2014] FCA 1191, involved the prosecution of John Holland following the death of a worker on the Perth City Rail project, an engineering project that involved sinking railway tracks. The worker was killed when a piece of equipment known as a *"hi-rail vehicle"* rolled out of control, down a decline striking the worker. The worker was using a high-pressure water and air hose to clean debris and dust from the rail tracks and was wearing hearing protection when he was hit by the vehicle.

In its decision, the Court noted:

> *Mr Cipolla referred to an audit carried out by the applicant during February and March 2013 of a number of the John Holland Group's operations including the City Rail project. The applicant's audit was to assess legislative compliance and effectiveness of the John Holland Group's safety policies, procedures and*

management systems. The audit report recorded, said Mr Cipolla, that out of 112 applicable criteria, there was 100% compliance by the John Holland Group. [33]

...

The respondents also pointed to Mr Cipolla's evidence of the respondents' longstanding and conscientious commitment to ensuring health and safety at the workplace, the promotion of a health and safety culture, and to the results of the applicant's audit. [88]

...

However, notwithstanding the laudable steps taken by the respondents in reducing the risk of serious accident arising from the on-tracking and off-tracking of a hi-rail vehicle, and the results of the applicant's audit, it is, still necessary, in my view, to include in the penalty, a substantial element in recognition of the need for specific deterrence. This is because, as is demonstrated by the facts of this case, the operation of an effective health and safety system at the workplace requires as Madgwick J said, "constant vigilance" and the need to adopt a proactive rather than a reactive approach to safety. [90]

Similar observations were made in a US Chemical Safety and Hazard Investigation Board case study of a flammable vapour incident at the Yerkes chemical plant in Buffalo, New York (US Chemical Safety and Hazard Investigation Board, 2010). The Board identified:

In November 2006, DuPont corporate performed a PSM audit of the DuPont Buffalo facility. DuPont awarded DuPont Buffalo a score of 99% on this audit, the highest score the auditor team had ever awarded a facility. The audit commended the Buffalo facility on their operating procedures and safe work practices and made no

89

recommendations to improve these programs. No recommendations were made for the Buffalo facility's MOC procedure for subtle changes, stating that "all systems comply."

Another DuPont audit was carried out in October 2009. This document commended DuPont Buffalo's PHA process. It stated that the PHA's were "very well managed and executed" and are of "consistently high quality." **These latest audits carried out by DuPont at the DuPont Buffalo facility missed many deficiencies that became apparent as a result of the November 9, 2010, incident.** (My emphasis added) (paragraph 4.9)

I think in audit we clearly see the interplay between the Safety Paradox and the Illusion of Safety. On the one hand, organisations see audits as being a good thing for safety, and good audit scores are a vindication of the organisation's safety management system. In most cases, however, there is very little if any correlation between audit scores and safe work practices. Audits typically look at systems and processes – is there a documented control system in place? Is there a method for reporting about health and safety? Is there a program of management inspections?

It is very rare for audits to consider how well the processes work on the ground or whether they actually are effective to manage hazards. It is less common still for audits to test the question raised by the Cole Inquiry; are our processes understood by workers in the field and are they relevant to their daily activities? (Inquest into the death of Cameron Brandt Cole, 2015, p. 24).

So, while we might think of audits as a good thing – and they have a role to play – when we start to equate good audit scores with good health and safety management, we are making unjustified assumptions and accepting a view of health and safety management which may have no foundation in reality. Audits, in a very real sense, can make a significant contribution to the Illusion of Safety because of the meaning we ascribed to them.

However, in many cases the audit process is problematic at a deeper level. While audits might misrepresent the actual state of health and safety and contribute to the Illusion of Safety, the process also extracts significant time and resources from the organisation – time and resources that could be far better spent paying attention to operational safety matters.

It is not uncommon for health and safety teams and line managers to be drawn out of operational work for weeks at a time – sometimes months – to collate information and documents for audits or accreditation processes. In many larger organisations the ongoing cycle of audits and accreditation requires the attention of a dedicated department. Financially and practically, the effort expended by organisations on audits and accreditation in the name of health and safety seem to be out of all proportion to the benefits gained and do nothing to connect the workers and the way work is performed to the safety expectations of the organisation.

As Power observes:

> *Undoubtedly, new games will emerge around these systems-driven audit processes. Forms of 'non-compliance compliance' and creative strategies of submitting to audit processes will frustrate the mission of audit. At the same time organisations may be encumbered with structures of auditability embodying performance measures which **increasingly do not correspond to the first order reality of practitioners' work**.* (My emphasis added) (Michael, 1996, p. 28)

I think this is of particular significance to health and safety. The more our processes are directed to achieving audit and accreditation outcomes, the more they are removed from day-to-day operations in the field. They have less and less connection to the workers' day-to-day reality.

Gregory Smith

TRAINING AND COMPETENCE

Training and competence is almost always highlighted as a failing in accident investigations and inquiries. My own recent experiences with training and competence processes have reinforced the overwhelmingly bureaucratic nature of much of what we do in the name of training and competence, and the complete disconnect of the process of training from purpose.

In my view, it is hard to overstate both the importance of training and competence to effective health and safety management, and the lack of real effort and energy that goes into ensuring workers are properly trained and competent to perform their roles. We can point to example after example where investigations and inquiries have criticised training and competence (See for example, Smith, 2016, Chapter 4), but for now, an example from the Esso Royal Commission will be enough. Esso had argued that their operators were well-trained and failed to deal with basic, well understood hazards on the day the incident. The Royal Commission took a different view, finding that the *"real cause"* of the disaster was training:

> *Notwithstanding the matters mentioned above, the conclusion is inevitable that the accident ... would not have occurred had appropriate steps being taken ... Those who were operating [Gas Plant 1] on 25 September 1998 did not have knowledge of the dangers associated with the loss of lean oil flow and did not take*

the steps necessary to avert those dangers. Nor did those charged with the supervision of the operations have the necessary knowledge and the steps taken by them were inappropriate. The lack of knowledge on the part of both operators and supervisors was directly attributable to a deficiency in their initial or subsequent training. Not only was there training inadequate, but there were no current operating procedures to guide them in dealing with the problems which they encountered on 25 September 1998. (Dawson & Brooks, 1999, p. 234)

Far from heed the lessons of history, it seems the knee-jerk response of the health and safety industry has been a *"more is better"* approach, pumping out more and more training, longer and more fulsome inductions (more and more *"process"*) facilitated by online or computer-based training or volumes of *"I have read and understood"* tick and flick reviews of safety procedures. All of this is evidenced by increasing levels of bureaucracy (i.e. paperwork). The important lessons, the quality of training, the level of retention, the level of understanding and implementation in the workforce have been left behind, or buried under ever expanding training matrices and verifications of competence.

I recently had to attend a mine site for two days, and the price of admission was to give up about three hours of my time and sit through an online, 165 slide PowerPoint presentation. Needless to say, I absorbed none of it, so to the extent that the organisation was hoping the process contributed to safety it was a pointless exercise. Equally, as the Harris decision (*Harris v Coles Supermarkets Australia Pty Ltd* [2017] ACTSC 81) illustrates, it would have provided very little comfort in the event of legal proceedings:

The defendant's induction package is lengthy and it covers many matters of employment, courtesy, health and safety issues, and the use of a great deal of equipment. Many of the items initialled by the plaintiff

94

appear irrelevant to her job, although she did recall "Dave" demonstrating to her use of the garbage compactor. She said she had no idea how to use items such as an electric pallet jack, which is one of the items she had initialled. She maintained she had never been shown in her induction or training how to use the safety step, but had merely followed another employee, and how that employee had been using the step. [40]

These findings are certainly consistent with my experience.

On another occasion I was working with a client and came across a *"Verification of Competence"* folder in the training room. The folder contained two, A4 pages with a list of safe working procedures on each page, back and front. In total there were more than 120 separate procedures. The worker had initialled against each procedure and signed the document to acknowledge he had *"read and understood"* the procedures.

There is nothing unusual about this, it is common practice, but of course it is complete nonsense, offering no evidence the worker actually reviewed the documents, much less understood them. It certainly offers no evidence of "competence". Again, we can see parallels with the Harris decision (*Harris v Coles Supermarkets Australia Pty Ltd* [2017] ACTSC 81):

The plaintiff had difficulty in recalling the exact nature of the training day, other than using butcher's paper and whiteboard markers and being asked to answer questions to work out solutions to problems. She frankly admitted that her memory of any training in 2009 was not as fresh now as it would have been then. She initialled a number of sheets of paper but could not recall much instruction being given. [11]

... She said she asked about some of the items listed on the forms and was told to "just initial it" as she was

needed on the floor and it would be "sorted out later".
[12]

I managed to track down the worker in the yard, who had the good grace to admit he flicked through *"about 20% of the documents"*, but could not really tell me what was in them, although he did not seem concerned about this because:

> *These sorts of procedures are the same everywhere you*
> *go anyway, aren't they?*

The lip service paid to safety and the bureaucratic paper chase which characterises training and competence in health and safety would be comical, if it were not so serious, and so widely accepted. Almost everyone I speak to accepts that induction processes are simply something we have to go through, and that the tick and flick sign off on reams of safe working and other procedures are not an effective way to achieve meaningful training outcomes. The lack of quality training in health and safety seems to be accelerating with the continual push for *"online training"*.

I think there is a role for online training. Indeed, I develop it myself, and recommend it to clients in some circumstances, but like the rest of health and safety management, we need to approach it with a level of critical thinking directed to achieving the purpose, not just to evidencing a process. The risk is that online training is such an effective tool at evidencing process that we lose sight of the purpose, and the lessons of history. The Baker Panel review into the BP Texas City Refinery explosion made important observations about online, or computer-based training which in my view are even more important today with the explosion in technology related applications for health and safety:

> *Computer-based training, while useful for informing*
> *personnel about changes and effective in teaching*
> *certain types of subject matter, is less effective at*

> *developing adequate process safety awareness and the skills and ability needed to apply knowledge in actual operations.* (Baker, et al., 2007, p. 164)

The number, or percentage of training programs completed is often a reported indicator of health and safety performance included, for example, in monthly health and safety reports. However, *"training completed"* is simply a measure of activity, it is an indicator of process and not an indicator of outcome, or whether the process has achieved its purpose. Again, when commenting on computer-based training, the Baker Panel review observed the lack of rigour in the training and its inability to actually assess worker knowledge:

> *For example, a 2001 root cause analysis report relating to an incident at the Toledo refinery involving an operator stated that the training system does not fully assess if a person has mastered the material being taught, noting that the operator in question passed a training test with a 100% score.*

> *Although employees must eventually pass the computer-based tests, BP's U.S. refineries commonly provided repeated opportunities for employees to retake the same tests if needed. Some employees suggested that these repeat opportunities were almost unlimited.* (Baker, et al., 2007, p. 164)

If there is one thing, over and above everything else, which I believe would have a real and lasting impact on health and safety performance, health and safety management and do more than anything else to protect the lives of workers and other people affected by business, it would be a significant, real and meaningful investment in training and competence. If we can only manage to remove bureaucracy from one area of health and safety management, this is where it should be.

WORKPLACE TOOLS

Workers are confronted with, and have to use, multiple documented processes, forms and checklists as part of their day-to-day work. Often, workers have to complete the same paperwork every day for routine tasks, creating frustration, disillusionment and disengagement. It seems at this point, where process and paperwork intersect most obviously, that bureaucracy is most commonly understood as, or equated to, paperwork.

It is here also that we see the paperwork process unravel from its intended purpose. Paperwork becomes a mechanistic form filling response where the intention is to complete the paperwork and get on with the job, rather than use the paperwork as a credible risk management and mitigation tool.

In 2010, a worker was killed during operations to install a 1.8 tonne, 14 m long steel beam. While the steel beam was being lifted by a crane the worker was standing under the load pulling on a tagline trying to lower one end of the beam. As the worker was doing this, the fabric sling supporting the steel beam snapped and the beam dropped on his head killing him. Although there were a range of bureaucratic documented processes designed to manage just this sort of risk, the process had clearly deteriorated to a *"paper system"*, that added very little if anything to the day-to-day management of risk:

> *At the day's pre-start toolbox meeting each employee was required to sign a "cover sheet" to the general JSA to acknowledge they were aware of it. Each employee*

*was also required to sign a general safety awareness document called a START card. This is an acronym for Stop, Think, Assess, Review and Talk. Whilst the START cards had space for specific hazard control measures to be added, nothing was noted about this lifting job. As described by the prosecutor, the signings were **primarily treated by both Ferro Con and the employees as a 'tick and flick' exercise**.*

...

*As indicated, a cover sheet to the structural steel erection JSA was signed daily, **largely as a perfunctory exercise to fulfil Adelaide Aqua's requirements.***

No detailed JSA's for different types of lifts, or lift plans, were required by Adelaide Aqua. Ferro Con took its cue for the level of safety planning it would use in its work from Adelaide Aqua, and not from the foreseeable hazards of its work activities. Ferro Con was more focussed on complying with contractual requirements than taking all reasonably practicable steps to minimise the foreseeable hazards its business created (my emphasis added) (Hillman v Ferro Con (SA) Pty Ltd (in Liquidation) and Anor [2013] SAIRC 22).

The notion of *"tick and flick"* is a clear marker of bureaucracy in safety management, and in my view the only reason it persists is because process has prevailed over purpose. Organisations are prepared to accept completed paperwork as evidence of outcome – evidence that what is represented on paper is a true reflection of workplace reality. This disconnect is compounded because the process – the completion of forms – becomes a measure of success, not the outcomes intended by the completion of the paperwork. Not the management of hazards.

I have already mentioned, based on several case examples, that it often appears documented safety processes are developed not for safety objectives but for other, bureaucratic requirements. In my experience, these bureaucratic requirements include:

- to meet audit requirements;

- to meet accreditation requirements;

- to comply with directions from health and safety regulators.

While the documented processes are developed – they are created – there is no plan and often no intention to incorporate these documents into existing safety processes or to inform the workforce about, or train them in, these processes. In many cases, the development of the processes are outsourced, and we have seen an entire industry of so called "*technical writing*" evolve of the back of health and safety bureaucracy.

In my experience, the development of process for its own sake is especially prevalent in contracting relationships. In these relationships the principal requires a contractor to develop health and safety tools, and the contractor develops them. I think it is a universal truth in health and safety that if a principal wants the contractor to give them something, the contractor will give them what they asked for. I think it is *almost* a universal truth that whatever the contractor gives the principal will have very little if any, influence over how the work is actually performed.

As demonstrated in the Ferro Con case, processes become a tick and flick exercise to meet some perceived bureaucratic requirement – in this case a contractual requirement – it does not have a connection to purpose.

The prevalence of bureaucracy in workplace tools is wide and varied, with the potential to affect all commonly used workplace tools. There are many examples of this in an Australian context, but I suspect these themes are universal. Examples include the Job Hazard Analysis, or JHA, the Safe Work Method Statement, or SWMS and checklists.

JHA

The JHA is a ubiquitous, workplace, frontline risk management tool used by organisations across Australia. It may operate under different names, such as JSEA (Job Safety Environmental Analysis), JSA (Job Safety Analysis), TRA (Task Risk Assessment), and so on.

The JHA is typically a *"team-based"* risk assessment. Before undertaking a task, a work team (in theory) will review the task, describe each of the steps in that task, the hazards associated with each step, and the controls to manage the hazards.

The philosophy behind the JHA is that workers will identify the health and safety risks associated with their activities, put in place controls to manage those health and safety risks, and then work in accordance with those controls.

Theoretically this makes sense. The reality is often very different. For what it is worth, in my view, the JHA is a tool uniquely unsuited to the people who have to use it. Many of our frontline workers are exceptionally talented in what they do, and undertake tasks on a daily basis that I could never hope to achieve. However, they are not interested in filling in forms, have questionable levels of literacy and comprehension and should not be asked to complete paperwork that is, ultimately, intended to provide some sort of defence in legal proceedings.

There is strong evidence to suggest that workers become focused on completing the paperwork at the expense of actually understanding the risks associated with their work. Moreover, many of these processes have degenerated into a mindless tick and flick exercise. Not only do these processes not add value to safety, they can actively undermine safety in the workplace by contributing to the *"illusion of safety"* (Borys, 2009, p. 7).

This has certainly been an experience evidenced in courts and inquiries, as we saw earlier in the Ferro Con case, where the JHA was one of several processes which were simply being done to meet contractual requirements and arguably distracted the organisation from properly understanding and managing the health and safety risks in their work.

These same issues have been proven in numerous cases. One example is a New South Wales District Court decision, *Inspector Nash v Perilya Broken Hill Limited* [2018] NSWDC 28.

On 8 June 2012, an employee of Perilya Broken Hill Limited (**PBHL**), Mr Pollard, suffered a traumatic amputation of his right leg and other injuries when he fell down a haulage shaft at a mine in Broken Hill (**Mine**). At the time of the incident Mr Pollard, was trying to hang some weights from the bottom of a weight flask to calibrate a load cell which measured the weight of ore in the flask.

The weights were in a metal basket and the weight Mr Pollard was hanging was about 10 tonnes. The weights and basket were in the bucket of a loader. Mr Pollard was trying to hang the weights by working from the bucket of the loader, the bucket being in the haulage shaft.

Mr Pollard was secured to the bucket by personal protective equipment (**PPE**), a fall arrest system comprising harness and lanyard. His lanyard was tied to the bucket.

Gregory Smith

While Mr Pollard was working, the weights and basket came out of the bucket and so did Mr Pollard. His lanyard snapped, and he fell.

The case canvassed a range of issues in safety management, including the role of the Job Safety Analysis (**JSA**).

One of the allegations pleaded by the prosecutor was PBHL failed to "*assess the adequacy of the Job Safety Analysis*".

The Court took its direction for what a JSA required from PBHLs own documents:

> *I start by looking at what is required of a JSA. This may be discerned in the first instance from the defendant's documents.*
>
> *What is required in a JSA is detail that shows:*
>
> - *how the hazards were identified;*
>
> - *how the risks were assessed;*
>
> - *how the decisions around necessary controls were made.* ([426] – [427])

The Broken Hill Job Safety Analysis Procedure had out six steps in the JSA process. They included:

- A JSA must be conducted in a team setting.

- A JSA should be done on the job site

- Task supervisors must ensure compliance with the requirements for a JSA.

None of these requirements were met.

PBHL's procedures said:

The success and value of the risk management process is determined by the quality of the consultation and communication process. Success hinges on involving the right people and using the right information, expertise and experience. Hence, identification and participation of stakeholders is critical. ([439])

The Court found that there was *"no consultation or communication with the correct stakeholders"* ([439]).

PBHL's procedures said:

The less formal nature of ... JSAs can present a serious risk in itself. It is essential that these tools are used carefully. If a significant or uncertain risk is missed or not properly managed, participants may be lulled into a false sense of security. Some things to look out for include:

- *New tasks or one that is being done in a new place or using a new method* ([440])

In relation to this, the Court said:

- *This was a new task using a new method. The "serious risk" warning should have been heeded* ([440]).

The Court closely examined PBHL's own requirements for its JSA process, ultimately finding the process to prepare the JSA was seriously flawed, the JSA itself was inadequate and:

The risk assessment did not involve all those doing the work and was not communicated to all of them. It stood the risk of being and was, for reasons I give, "next to worthless" ([441]).

104

It is worth noting, the Court's use of the term *"worthless"* is not random. The Court has adopted the language of *"worthless"* from PBHL's own documents.

PBHL's Risk Management Guideline gave several directions about risk management, for example:

> *A risk assessment is worthless if it does not involve communicating with the correct stakeholders* ([439]).

And

> *Ultimately a risk assessment is next to worthless if it is done in isolation without involving those doing the work, or not communicated to all those doing the work or affected by the work* ([441]).

The Court did not have to look for language to criticise the JSA process, it simply adopted PBHL's own views.

PBHL employees accepted the inadequacy of the JSA, for example, a supervisor, Mr Harris:

> *... agreed that it was not appropriate for one person to simply to write out a JSA and then present it to others without those persons having input into its development. He agreed that a JSA should be prepared as a team, particularly as some members of the team may not be aware of, or understand each of the steps of the task. He noted that this was an important consideration, particularly as there might be persons with different subject expertise performing various parts of the task. He also agreed that it would be important to have all members of the team involved in completing a JSA because if only one person completed the JSA, there was a risk that a step would be missed in the process, or a*

hazard missed or an appropriate control measure not identified ([443]).

Not only does this case demonstrate the potential bureaucratisation of health and safety – the disconnect between process and purpose, it also shows the phenomena of bureaucratic "*layering*" in health and safety management systems.

What we see in the Perilya decision is a bureaucratic procedure, using subjective and emotive terminology – worthless – which adds no value to safety, used to compound the failure to implement a process.

Organisations are accountable for what they say in their documented processes. If you are going to describe an in-depth, potentially convoluted process for preparing documents like JSAs, you need to recognise you are prescribing the standard against which you will be measured. Write your documents with the end user in mind to give workers some chance of following them.

Regardless of what you document, you need to understand if it is implemented and effective. It is extremely unlikely this case was the first time the JSA procedure was ignored in so many fundamental ways. The history of workplace accidents in Australia is compelling – frontline risk assessment documents like JSAs have little meaning to frontline workers and are often seen as an exercise in bureaucracy: A paper process workers have to complete before the work can commence.

In my mind, the JHA is a particularly acute example of bureaucracy in safety management, and one that organisations should be paying much closer attention to. Historically, the JHA is used to control high-risk work activities, and in workplaces where JHAs are used, no high-risk work activity can be performed without doing a JHA.

Gregory Smith

When I refer to high-risk work activities, I am referring to work such as working at height, work in confined spaces, excavation work, certain isolations and some electrical work.

If you have a process in your workplace that is mandatory for all high-risk work activities, surely that process becomes a *"critical"* process? Surely, you have some positive obligation to understand if that process is effective?

History would tend to suggest that at best, organisations have an understanding about whether JHA's are *done* by workers. History would tend to suggest that organisations have no understanding about whether their JHA process is *effective* to achieve the outcomes it is designed to achieve – indeed history would suggest organisations have no clear articulation of the outcomes JHAs are designed to achieve, and never ask the question whether they are effective.

The question that comes out of a decision like the Perilya case has nothing to do with Perilya. The question is, how do you know that your JSA procedures are any better in practice?

Safe Work Method Statements

Unlike the JHA, Safe Work Method Statements are a product of legislation in Australia. They are required by law in certain circumstances.

Like the JHA however, they have been hijacked by health and safety and turned into a trivial nonsense with very little meaning for workers.

Safe Work Method Statements are required for a very limited range of work activities. Typically, they are required for high risk construction work. For example, the *Work Health and Safety*

Regulations 2011 (NSW), regulation 299 states that a Safe Work Method Statement must be prepared for high risk construction work.

High risk construction work is defined:

In this Chapter, high risk construction work means construction work that:

(a) involves a risk of a person falling more than 2 metres, or

(b) is carried out on a telecommunication tower, or

(c) involves demolition of an element of a structure that is load-bearing or otherwise related to the physical integrity of the structure, or

(d) involves, or is likely to involve, the disturbance of asbestos, or

(e) involves structural alterations or repairs that require temporary support to prevent collapse, or

(f) is carried out in or near a confined space, or

(g) is carried out in or near:

> *(i) a shaft or trench with an excavated depth greater than 1.5 metres, or*

> *(ii) a tunnel, or*

(h) involves the use of explosives, or

(i) is carried out on or near pressurised gas distribution mains or piping, or

(j) is carried out on or near chemical, fuel or refrigerant lines, or

(k) is carried out on or near energised electrical installations or services, or

(l) is carried out in an area that may have a contaminated or flammable atmosphere, or

(m) involves tilt-up or precast concrete, or

(n) is carried out on, in or adjacent to a road, railway, shipping lane or other traffic corridor that is in use by traffic other than pedestrians, or

(o) is carried out in an area at a workplace in which there is any movement of powered mobile plant, or

(p) is carried out in an area in which there are artificial extremes of temperature, or

(q) is carried out in or near water or other liquid that involves a risk of drowning, or

(r) involves diving work.

Safe Work Method Statements are potentially an important tool for managing high risk tasks. Unfortunately, health and safety has decided that if they are good for high risk tasks, they must be good for everything. Safe Work Method Statements have become a commoditised product being sold for all manner of work, from cleaning public park amenities, or removing graffiti to cleaning offices and removing rubbish.

None of these activities need a Safe Work Method Statement, and all we achieve by adding them to the pile of paperwork is to create more confusion, add to the *"initiative overload"* and diminish the importance of Safe Work Method Statements for the critical, high risk activities.

Is it any wonder that health and safety is the subject of derision when we stand up in front of organisations and argue that multipage documents and checklists are required for essentially benign activities, and completely corrupt the important and necessary principles behind managing high risk activities?

Is it any wonder that workers do not see the value in these documents when they must complete them for all manner of work?

The love affair with the unnecessary Safe Work Method Statement seems to have enamoured even regulators and prosecutors. In *Safe Work NSW v Wollongong Glass P/L* [2016] NSWDC 58, a decision I referred to earlier, a worker was killed when they were crushed under the weight of several glass panels.

In the case, the Court accepted the employer had a system of work, though it was not *"reduced to writing"*. The employer implemented their system of work through verbal direction and on-the-job training, enforced by supervision. The prosecution alleged there were a range of reasonably practicable steps the employer could have taken, and the steps were proven because they were adopted by the employer *after* the accident in a Safe Work Method Statement.

Ultimately, the Court accepted that the employer's system of work was sufficient, notwithstanding it was not a written system. The Court found the system of work provided adequate training, including the use of a buddy system, which was enforced by supervision.

Moreover, the Court expressly found:

> *It was not reasonably practicable for the defendant to provide the training required by sub-paragraph 6(a) and 6(d) in a written SWMS for the following reasons.*
>
> *First, a SWMS is only required by the regulations for "high risk construction work", which the work in the factory was not ...* ([95] – [96]).

In many respects, it appears that making a Safe Work Method Statement a regulatory requirement creates more harm than benefit. Many of the cases suggest Safe Work Method Statements are being put in place to meet a bureaucratic requirement imposed by legislation, regardless of whether the Safe Work Method Statement is the best way to manage risk, or even correctly addresses the relevant risk at all.

In the Wollongong Glass case, the Court went on to observe:

> *... while a SWMS may provide evidence that a defendant has in place a safe work procedure, does not necessarily follow that its workers have been adequately trained in the content of a SWMS or that they will comply with it. Both Mr Pham and Mr Heaton were considered to be good workers. Neither of them could read the SWMS that was adopted on 14 March 2013.* [98]

Here again we see, arguably, a bureaucratic requirement on the one hand – implement a Safe Work Method Statement – balanced against the need to manage health and safety risk. In many cases, the Safe Work Method Statement will be the least effective approach to managing health and safety risk, and blind adherence to a regulatory requirement is likely to make the workplace less, not more, safe.

Even where a Safe Work Method Statement is required, we still see ample evidence of the *"process"* of Safe Work Method Statement development and documentation being disconnected from the purpose it is designed for – the management of risk in the workplace.

In a 2017 case, *Safe Work (NSW) v Action Concreting and Constructions Pty Ltd [2017] NSWDC 191*, a worker was seriously injured when they fell from height, but again the documented procedures to manage that risk were of little comfort to the company:

> *Kazoo had in place a safe work method statement (SWMS) relating to working at heights in general terms. The SWMS was not site-specific and had been developed in relation to previous jobs carried out on other sites.*
>
> *The SWMS addressed the risk of falling under the activity heading "Working at Height" and identified scaffolding as the applicable control measure for this activity. Site-specific risks and the measures to eliminate them had not been explained to the workers on the site. The SWMS did not provide any guidance on the steps required to eliminate or minimise the risk of falling over the edge of the first floor. No system existed to ensure that the SWMS was followed when undertaking the work. No comprehensive training had been provided to the workers at the site in relation to the risks of working at height and how to reduce or minimise the risk of falling from a height.*
>
> *The work was not conducted in accordance with the SWMS.*

Checklists

Checklists are a very common workplace health and safety management tool. They are used for all manner of activity from prestart checks on large mobile plant to light vehicle inspections.

Gregory Smith

However, history has clearly demonstrated checklists can become a burden on the workforce which get ignored or dealt with in a cursory tick and flick manner.

For example, a checklist was used as part of the procedures before restarting operations at BP Texas City:

> *A functionality check of all alarms and instruments was also required prior to startup, but these checks were not completed. On March 22, 2005, instrument technicians had begun checking the critical alarms when a supervisor told them that the unit was starting up and there was no time for additional checks.*
>
> *While some alarms were tested, most were not prior to startup. The supervisor, however, initialed on the startup procedure that those checks had been completed* (U.S. Chemical Safety and Hazard Investigation Board, 2007, pp. 48 - 49).

Similarly, a Queensland coroner's inquiry (Non-inquest findings into the deaths of Jamie Christopher ADAMS and Gary Robert WATKINS, 2018, p. 8) which considered a daily service check on a vehicle, found:

> *Operating crew members stated to the Queensland Transport investigator that a complete adherence to the checklist was time-consuming. Consequently, the usual practice was for a random crew member to conduct cursory checks only on the key items relating to lubrication, calling and work had mechanisms. The entire checklist would then usually be marked to indicate compliance.*
>
> *I agree with the Queensland Transport investigator who was of the view that this "tick and flick" practice, over time, eroded the assurance that was intended to be provided by the checklist. It permitted a technically*

unserviceable Track Machine to operate in work mode within a work site. ... It is my view that this failure is likely to have contributed to the deaths of Mr Adams and Mr Watkins.

I am not arguing these processes – JHA, Safe Work Method Statement or checklists – are unnecessary or unimportant. They may be very necessary. They may be very important.

What I am arguing is the danger of assuming these processes are achieving their purpose.

First, I am asking organisations to recognise bureaucracy might impact on the effectiveness of their safety management systems.

Second, I am asking organisations to recognise that just because paperwork is completed , does not mean it is achieving its designed "*purpose*" – it does not mean that risk is being managed. And if an organisation is prepared to recognise these two possibilities, might we ask different questions about the way we go about work?

Is it necessary to do a JHA for every task? Do we really need a Safe Work Method Statement for activities other than high risk construction work? Do I need to do a vehicle inspection checklist every day?

If it is necessary to do these things? If the paperwork is important, then is it treated with the importance it deserves? Can we at least commit to a robust meaningful management effort to review and analyse the paperwork we are asking workers to generate? Can we at least commit to being satisfied that in addition to being done, the paperwork is achieving the purpose for which it was designed?

Gregory Smith

Another phenomenon that characterises health and safety bureaucracy is the need to "*keep*" health and safety documents.

You would think, having created, collected and stored huge quantities of historical health and safety documentation, there would be ongoing and concerted efforts to review that documentation to ensure it was being completed correctly and analyse the information to learn as much as possible about how well health and safety risks were being managed.

This does not seem to be the case.

My impression of safety management systems over the last 20 plus years is of highly documented, bureaucratic processes that workers do not understand, replete with documents that are very poorly completed then collected and stored. This process effectively expends an extraordinary amount of an organisation's resources and energy on building databases to show the extent to which the organisation does not comply with its own systems, but at the same time seeming to have – at least not in a way that can be demonstrated – very little positive influence on safety outcomes.

The creation of databases demonstrating non-compliance is compounded because nobody ever analyses the information. Great swathes of information about the efficacy of our safety management systems and the extent to which people comply with them reside in our organisations, but the only people who ever read and analyse the information is lawyers and regulators after an accident.

If we actually took time to analyse the mass of information sitting in safety management databases, more often than not it will provide very meaningful insight into the state of our safety management systems. Some examples that I have come across over the years areset out below.

Take 5's Version 1

I came across this case when a medium-sized mining company called me to help them following a serious workplace accident.

One of the first things I do when I work with organisations, either proactively or reactively (i.e. helping to set up systems or responding to accidents) is try and understand the processes they have in place to manage the health and safety risks in their business. When I am dealing with an accident, I try to understand the processes that were in place to manage the specific hazards giving rise to the incident and then analyse those processes to understand how well implemented they were before the incident.

In this case, I was looking at the Take 5 process as one of the elements of the process designed to prevent the incident.

A Take 5 process is a checklist or risk assessment that an individual worker completes just before they commence a task. The theory behind the document is that it prompts the worker to take a few moments (i.e. five minutes) to stop and think about the health and safety hazards associated with their work before they commence. In this case, the Take 5 also had a risk ranking component and the workers had to assign a numerical value to the risk of the work they were performing. This was done using a standard 5 x 5 risk matrix and was based on a combination of consequence (what's the worst thing that could happen if something goes wrong) and likelihood (how likely is it that something will go wrong).

In this case, the organisation had a process whereby every time a work order was issued to workers, they had to do a Take 5, and the Take 5 had to be stapled to the work order, which was then filed.

Gregory Smith

The work orders and their associated Take 5 were filed in black lever arch files and kept in a five-tier bookshelf in the main administration office on site. The bookshelf ran between the General Manager's office and the Health and Safety Manager's office. At the time there were three years' worth of work orders and Take 5's stored in the bookshelf.

To understand whether this process of work orders and Take 5 was well implemented and effective we reviewed all the available documents – three years' worth.

On the plus side, every work order had a Take 5 attached. There was clearly a high level of compliance with the *process*.

Less encouraging was the fact that in 97% of the cases, the Take 5 had a risk score of 21. This, on its face was highly improbable. The idea that 97% of tasks completed on a mine site in a three-year period would all have the same risk ranking seemed far-fetched. However, the scores made perfect sense in the light of the safety processes. The problem was that if the Take 5 had a risk score of 22, then you had to do a JHA for the task. This meant the reward for properly completing one piece of paperwork was to be able to complete another, more extensive piece of paperwork.

The workforce was very quick to admit, both to us and to the regulator, that they all scored their Take 5, 21 so they did not have to do the JHA.

This, of itself, was not evidence that people on the site did not work safely. Indeed, apart from the incident in question they had a very good safety record. But it does mean that it was almost impossible to present a case to the regulator that there was an effective, well implemented system of Take 5 on their site.

Further, because nobody had taken the time to aggregate and analyse the information being generated by the Take 5 process, all the organisation had managed to do was to produce a significant database demonstrating non-compliance with their own system. If anybody had paid proper attention to the Take 5 process, it would have been immediately apparent that it was not operating as intended, and indeed it was being manipulated to avoid what the organisation had described as other, important safety processes.

Take 5's version 2

I came across another example of the Take 5 process when I was asked to do a review of safety management during a construction project on a mine site.

In this case, each worker was asked to complete at least one Take 5 every day, all of which were collected at the end of the shift. The health and safety administration office on the site was located near the parking bay for the buses, and each evening, the workers would walk past the health and safety administration office to catch the bus back to the accommodation village. Outside of the health and safety administration office was a box, and the workers put their Take 5 into that box on the way to catch the bus.

There was a woman who worked in the health and safety administration office on an "*8 and 6*" swing. This meant that she spent 8 days on-site and 6 days at home. Typically, the first 3 days of her swing (i.e. time on site) was spent scanning and uploading the Take 5s into a database. The number of Take 5s in the database was compared to the workers on site and a percentage was generated. At the time I was doing my review, compliance was running at about 98%, meaning that almost every worker completed a Take 5 every day and dropped it into the box outside of the health and safety administration office.

Gregory Smith

As part of my review, I looked at 750 Take 5s. Not one of them had been done correctly.

The Take 5 was a two-sided document that needed a date and a signature. In many cases workers did not date the documents. In others they were not signed. In other cases, workers only filled out one side of the document, or the checklist had not been completed, or comments not added.

Whatever the missing element, not one of the Take 5 documents had been done correctly.

The effect of this, or so it seemed to me, was the organisation was paying a person three days a week to produce a database of non-compliance with their system.

What made this worse, in my view, was that the 98% "*compliance*" score meant that the Take 5 – as an indicator of safety – had a green "*traffic light*" in the monthly health and safety report. This green traffic light was interpreted by management as meaning that the Take 5 system worked, and with an even broader leap of faith, that people were working safely.

The Take 5 system did not work, and even if it did, this is not proof people are working safely.

Once again, it seems to me that if anybody had bothered to analyse this extensive database it would have been immediately apparent that the Take 5 process was not operating as intended, and moreover their health and safety reporting was fundamentally misleading and a dangerous illusion of safety.

INCIDENT INVESTIGATIONS

Incident investigations are particularly interesting in the context of health and safety management systems. I would not deny they are important to effective health and safety management, but at the same time they take up a lot of time, effort and energy within an organisation. It also seems to me, that incident investigations are used retrospectively on a "*one-off*" basis. By that, I mean organisations will conduct an incident investigation and use it to understand the circumstances of that *particular* incident. The incident investigation itself will be judged as "*good*" or "*bad*" as a standalone document.

Whenever I run management training or incident investigation training I asked the question, "*does your system of incident investigation work*", and the answer is inevitably, "*investigations work if they are done well*".

This misses the point of the question. If we are going to go to the trouble of conducting incident investigations, compiling the findings, recording the findings in a database and ultimately keeping all these incident investigations, isn't it incumbent on us to understand if the process of incident investigations work?

However, you define incident investigations, if indeed you do, in most organisations, incident investigations:

a. Have become a bureaucratic exercise, contorting factual findings to fit a predetermined set of criteria; and

b. Are measured against markers of activity.

Let me explain.

Many commercially available incident investigation models are based on a linear, causal chain. Some common examples include ICAM (see for example: www.safetywise.com), TapRoot (see for example: http://www.taproot.com), Kelvin Top Set (see for example: http://www.kelvintopset.com).

Most models describe categories of information to help an investigator collect data. For example, they will describe what information an investigator should ask about people, or equipment, or procedures and so on. Once data is collected and a factual chain of events is described, various factors are ascribed *"causal'* or *"contributory"* status and classified according to a pre-determined set of classification criteria. Classification criteria often include things such as organisational factors, individual or team actions, and management systems. Many models will have layers of subsets of the criteria. The biggest challenge for many incident investigators applying these models is wading through the plethora of criteria to determine the correct one.

Of course, in an organisation were incident investigations are important, and not just a bureaucratic exercise, the allocation of *"causal factors"* is an extensive, time-consuming exercise. In many organisations were incident investigations are forced onto middle managers and supervisors, it is a simple *"tick a box"* exercise to complete the investigation as soon as possible.

Like all initiatives for health and safety, incident investigation methodologies can be useful, but they also have the capacity to undermine safety and health - the Safety Paradox.

On the one hand, mandatory investigation models provide a consistent framework for investigating incidents in an organisation. Theoretically, this means if incidents are properly investigated using the methodology (a big assumption and one that organisations do not test) organisations should be able to identify trends or systemic failure in safety management. By consistently classifying causal factors in incidents the same way, organisations should be able to understand contributors to workplace incidents.

However, investigation models which use set, causal classifications have been criticised as too restrictive, potentially undermining the efficacy of investigations.

Professor Trevor Kletz (Kletz, 2001, p. 7), describes it this way:

> *Personally I have not found such models useful. I find that time may be spent struggling to fit the data into the framework and that this distracts from the free-ranging thinking required to uncover the less obvious ways of preventing the accident. ... Use models by all means if you find them useful but do not become a slave to them. Disregard them if you find that they are not helping you.*

The Baker Panel Review into the BP Texas City refinery disaster (Baker, et al., 2007, p. 199) had this to say about BP's *"comprehensive list of causes"* methodology:

> *A major concern associated with a checklist approach like the CLC is that users likely will not identify any factors other than those on the list. In the Panel's experience, investigations typically use a checklist as a complete list of potential causes instead of a starting*

point for discussion of the deeper root causes and usually will not identify factors that are not on the list. Labeling the list as "comprehensive" likely exacerbates this problem. The Panel also believes that BP's list of systemic factors related to engineering problems (e.g., "inadequate technical design") appears somewhat superficial. While inadequate technical design is a valid factor, BP should use it to invite more extensive inquiry: What is the design inadequacy? Why was it present? Why was it not discovered prior to the incident under investigation?

Here we see the tension between useful process, and bureaucracy disconnected from purpose. If we are using an investigation model for administrative convenience without critically analysing the model against changing needs and the purpose of incident investigation, our incident investigation process has become bureaucratic. It is being done to follow the process, rather than to achieve a purpose.

But even within the application of investigation models, bureaucracy can infect the process.

As I said earlier, by consistently classifying causal factors in incidents the same way, organisations should be able to understand the contributors to workplace incidents. Theoretically, these factors can be entered into a database and analysed to demonstrate trends and systemic weaknesses.

Except that is not what happens.

In most cases, incident investigation databases are simply a repository of system failure which give no useful insights into the efficacy of safety management. There is no effective analysis of the classified causes to understand what they tell us about the systems. In my experience, any attempt to analyse the causal or contributory factors creates further problems, because it is very difficult to determine the basis upon which they were classified in the first place. Again, this evidences that investigation teams are simply going through the process – finding classification for factor, rather than a meaningful exercise in understanding the incident.

Indeed, we can go one step further, and say these databases of historical causes and contributing factors create significant legal risk. They show repeat and systemic failure in circumstances where organisations have no systemic response.

Organisations will respond individually to each investigation, but not review the systemic issues.

This bureaucratic approach generated by predetermined methodologies and procedures compromise safety and create legal risk. More often than not, because incident investigations are bureaucratic processes, the database of incident investigations is not helpful to manage health and safety risk and can be used against the organisation following an accident.

An example of this in practice is a case referred to earlier, *Harris v Coles Supermarkets Australia Pty Ltd* [2017] ACTSC 81.

On 7 December 2009, a worker was injured at work while using a *"safety step"*. As she was stepping down from the safety step, her right ankle rolled, and she fell suffering injury to her right hip, ankle, knee, and shoulder. Ultimately, she was awarded more than $1 million in damages.

The Harris decision looked at the question of training and the use of the safety step, but it also had something to say about incident analysis:

> *An analysis of incidents involving use of the safety step*
> *at Coles stores across Australia was tendered. This was*

set out in a spreadsheet and covers the years 2004 to 2009, 385 incidents are noted.   On perusal of the spreadsheet, a wide variety of incidents are set out with a description of the incident and any injuries sustained. All of these are very brief and very imprecise.

... Some of the incidents relate to injuries stepping off the safety step, however it is all so imprecise as to be of little utility, other than to demonstrate that this step does cause problems for some of the workers and injury has resulted from its use. ([36] – [37])

In my view, it is not difficult to conclude incident investigation in this context is bureaucratic, simply going through the motions to comply with a *process*. There is nothing to suggest a clear *purpose* behind the incident investigations, or the extent to which the *purpose* was driving the *process*.

If you want to test this for yourself, look for the most common causal or contributory factor in your incident investigation database, for example *"inadequate training"*, or *"inadequate procedures"*, or *"procedure not used/not followed"*, or *"procedure followed incorrectly"*.

Ask yourself, has there been any systemic review and report about that factor? For example, if a common causal or contributory factor is *"procedure not followed"*, has there been a detailed analysis of why this is an issue in your organisation, not just in the context of specific incidents?

If there is no systemic review and report about common causal or contributory factors, it is a good indication that your processes have been hijacked by bureaucracy, and your organisation is simply going through the motions to comply with the process.

By far, the most common reporting metrics for incident investigations are things like:

a. The number of investigations completed within prescribed time frames; or

b. The percentage of corrective actions completed or closed out by the due date.

These are measures of activity. They tell us if things have been done. They tell us if the process has been complied with. They do not tell us if our investigations have been done well. They do not tell us if our corrective actions have been well implemented.

They do not tell us if purpose has been achieved.

We are measuring compliance against process, not achievement of purpose.

Organisations do not measure or report about incident investigations in terms of the *purpose*. What is the purpose of doing incident investigations in your organisation and does your system of incident investigation achieve the purpose?

Whatever beliefs may exist in organisations about the incident investigation processes, the evidence is strong that investigations are a bureaucratic processes and working through the mechanics of the methodology has become more important than the quality of, and learning from, the process.

Again, if this sounds like a harsh judgement, look for yourself. On the one hand, where in your organisation is there:

a. A statement setting out the purpose of your incident investigation process?

Gregory Smith

b. A regular and concise report or update about whether, or to what extent, your organisation is achieving that purpose?

Alternatively, to what extent is reporting about incident investigations characterised by measurements of activity? Things that were done? To me, it is self-evident that the more we focus on process over purpose, the more bureaucratic our systems are.

An example of a possible disconnect between process and purpose in the context of incident investigations emerges from the Royal Commission into the Pike River Coal Mine Disaster (Panckhurst, Bell, & Henry, 2012).

On 19 November 2010, catastrophic explosion occurred at the Pike River underground coal mine in New Zealand. 29 men died in the disaster, and the New Zealand government instigated a Royal Commission to investigate the causes of the disaster (Panckhurst, Bell, & Henry, 2012, Vol 1, p. 6 - 9).

One of the topics covered in the Royal Commission was the efficacy of incident investigations at Pike River prior to the explosion:

> *Pike had an incident/accident reporting and investigation system in place. Workers were required to report events on a report form. These forms went to the safety and training department. Mr Rockhouse investigated some serious matters himself. Otherwise investigations were undertaken by a manager or staff member from the appropriate department. Some events were investigated by a team, which could include the mine manager.*
>
> *The workers reported many incidents and accidents. The commission analysed 1083 reports and summarised a selection of 436 in a schedule. The schedule groups events by type, including methane spikes, ventilation,*

strata, bypassing, equipment sparking and a number of others. The numbers suggest that the workforce, including contractors, were committed to reporting events, though the extent of non-reporting is unknown. The reports certainly contained a wealth of information which, if properly analysed, revealed much about the systems and conduct underground.

However, there were problems with the investigation process. Many reports were assigned to an investigator, but no investigation was completed. This was evident from the report forms filed with the commission. Mr Couchman described the extent of this problem. Some departments would have only a handful of investigations outstanding, while the engineering and production departments sometimes had up to 70 uncompleted investigations and some were over a year old. Measures to deal with the backlog were unsuccessful. When the backlog was discussed with Mr White in October 2010 he decided that they should be cleared and a fresh start made 'with a new management and a new mine manager.' This meant that the incidents were never properly investigated.

The site health and safety committee reviewed a selection of incident/accident reports at its monthly meetings. Approximately six of these were selected at random, and a committee member assessed whether stipulated remedial actions had been carried out. If not, the incidents were reopened and followed up.

There was some trend analysis of, and action was taken on, some issues, such as contraband. But because reports were not analysed systematically for recurring safety problems, or weaknesses in control measures, many matters were not discovered. In this way potential information about safety and emerging risks was lost, and information that could have been obtained from completed investigations was not put to best use. The extent of this deficit was most apparent when Mr Rockhouse described his reaction to seeing the schedules prepared by the commission:

'Mr Wilding, when you spent that three days with me and you showed me that stuff you had me reduced to tears. I know there was no analysis like you've done with that [information] at Pike River.'

There was also a breakdown in providing feedback to the report writers. Mr Couchman considered there was no established system for providing feedback. Mr Rockhouse understood that when an investigation was completed, there should have been feedback to the reporter but this 'didn't happen'. (Panckhurst, Bell, & Henry, 2012, Vol 2, p. 76 - 77)

There is a very clear sense here, of simply going through the motions. This played out to a greater degree during cross examination of managers about the investigation process and various incident investigations:

Q.   *That incident accident form, I wonder if I could have it up please, Ms Basher. DAO.001.00359 [page]15.*

WITNESS   REFERRED   TO   DOCUMENT DAO.001.00359[page]15

Q.   *That's the 5th of October incident. It's got that same number in the top corner there, and then 16 please, Ms Basher. That summarises the auxiliary fan blade being sheared off and so on. Do you see that Mr White?*

A.   *Yeah.*

Q.   Seventeen, there's the event set out in some detail, [page] 17 please Ms Basher.

A.   Yep.

Q.   And then two pages on, [page]19, just the page in between seems to be a complete blank, "Discussion topics", and I just want to look at the list of improvements, these are matters that had to be worked on as a result of this incident, were they?

A.   Yes, they were.

Q.   First one, "Lack of working communication devices underground." What devices are we talking about and what was done to solve that problem?

A.   I'm not entirely sure what communication devices they're talking about, whether it was phones, DACs or gas monitoring, it doesn't make it clear enough in there to say what actual communication devices they're talking about.

Q.   Well, you saw this – presumably you saw this accident –

A.   Yes, I did see this accident report, yeah.

Q.   And you would've done the sign off on this one?

A.   I did and sent it on to the Department of Labour.

Q.   So wouldn't you have inquired into what was not working underground in terms of communication devices?

Gregory Smith

> *A.* *I may well have done at the time Mr Hampton, I can't remember.*
>
> *Q.* *"Lack of communication to the surface fan." What was done to rectify that?*
>
> *A.* *Again I can't remember what communication they're talking about, whether that would be telemetric or whatever. These recommendations were handled by the electrical engineering department. I can't sit here and confirm which ones were done and which weren't done.*
>
> *Q.* *Well, as mine manager isn't that your responsibility to find out what was being done and what wasn't being done? Weren't you the man responsible.* (Transcript of Phase Three Hearing Commencing 13 February 2012 at Greymouth, 2012, pp. 5040 - 5042)

Although the question was not directly asked, and the issue was not addressed in terms of *bureaucracy* in the Royal Commission, the types of issues raised are common in many incident investigations. For example, it is not unusual for an incident investigation to make a statement that does not fully explain its subject matter, such as:

> *"Lack of working communication devices underground."*

The fact that this type of ambiguous statement is not picked up and addressed in an investigation, or the investigation is not amended, is entirely consistent with the investigation being bureaucratic – a process the organisation is just working through. It is less easy to explain if the organisation was genuinely concerned about the purpose of the investigation and making sure investigations provide the best possible insight into incidents and the efficacy of safety management.

HEALTH AND SAFETY REPORTING

T he trend towards reporting compliance against bureaucratic requirements leads people to make misleading and dangerous assumptions about the state of health and safety management in an organisation, based on the health and safety reports.

Often, when people look to criticise health and safety reporting, they point to lag indicators such as injury rates. I do not want to focus on injury rates as a measure, but I would say that injury rate data is not a reliable indicator of health and safety performance:

> *The statistical information provided to the board on health and safety comprised mainly personal injury rates and time lost through accidents ...* **The information gave the board some insight but was not much help in assessing the risks of a catastrophic event faced by high hazard industries**. *... The board appears to have received no information* **proving the effectiveness** *of crucial systems such as gas monitoring and ventilation* (my emphasis added) (Panckhurst, Bell, & Henry, 2012).

There are no major accident inquiries that have identified personal injury rates as a legitimate measure of the effectiveness of health and safety management. Personal injury rates are a measure

132

of how many personal injuries have occurred – no more. Any organisation that assumes personal injury rates are a measure of the effectiveness of their safety management system is misguided. We have known this for decades.

Health and safety reporting is not about managing personal injury rates. Health and safety reporting should prove the effectiveness of our crucial systems for managing health and safety risk. If our systems are effective to manage health and safety risks, improved safety performance should follow. However, the reverse does not hold true, and countless major accident enquiries have identified fundamentally flawed safety management systems disguised by good and improving personal injury rates.

We have seen over time the development of so-called "*lead*" indicators as a counterpoint to traditional, lag indicators. Lead indicators our supposed to provide insight into the effectiveness of safety management systems.

But do they?

It seems more likely that lead indicators are no more than a measurement of compliance with our bureaucratic requirements, in other words, compliance with process.

Overwhelmingly, lead indicators are nothing more than a measure of activity and the fact that our measures of activity have 100% compliance – they are all green – creates a dangerous illusion of safety.

A popular "*lead*" indicator for safety and health is the number of management interactions. These might be variously described as safety conversations, safe act observations, behavioural observations, safety interactions, management walk arounds and so on. Inevitably, they show up in a health and safety report as part of a table of lead indicators or a dashboard of "*traffic lights*". These indicators, or traffic lights, are usually coloured red if the indicator has not been met, amber if it has not been completely met and green if the requirement has been met.

Other, typical indicators might include:

- Corrective actions closed;

- Audits completed;

- Training completed;

- Hazards identified; or

- Pre-start or "Take 5" cards completed.

No doubt there are countless more.

The difficulty with all of these indicators is that they are measures of *"activity"*. Invariably, they tell us whether things have been *"done"*

They tell us nothing about the quality or effectiveness of the activity.

They tell us nothing about the influence of the activity on safety.

They make no contribution to proving the effectiveness of our crucial systems.

Health and safety reporting seems to have no consciousness or awareness of concepts such as the Safety Paradox or the Illusion of Safety. Indeed, health and safety reporting plays a significant role in contributing to the Illusion of Safety.

Gregory Smith

I have already talked about the JHA in the context of becoming a bureaucratic process but reporting about the JHA is also bureaucratic in so far as it reports on activity (i.e. process) not whether the process is effective (i.e. purpose).

As I have discussed earlier, the JHA is a ubiquitous frontline risk assessment tool implemented by organisations all over the world. At its best, it can be an effective mechanism to help frontline workers identify the risks associated with their work and develop suitable controls to manage those risks. Conversely, it can also disengage the workforce from the safety management message of the organisation and drive a complete *"us and them"* mentality (the Safety Paradox).

Research suggests that significant numbers of workers see frontline risk assessment tools like the JHA as a backside covering exercise, designed to protect managers from legal risk in the event of an accident (Borys, 2009). In most workplaces, this idea does not come as a complete shock, and there is a general acceptance of the limits or weaknesses inherent in the JHA. However, the use of the JHA continues to roll on without analysis, without thought, without critical thinking and certainly without any reporting at a managerial level about its effectiveness.

I have never seen a health and safety report that provides information to the executive about the *effectiveness* of the JHA system in the business. Given that the JHA is one of the most critical tools used by organisations for the management of high-risk activities (including working at heights, confined space entry, lifting operations and so on) I find this extraordinary.

I am not going to advocate whether organisations should use a JHA. But I do not think there could be any reasonable argument for an organisation not to know whether their use of the JHA is beneficial to safety or is undermining it.

What about management interactions? As I indicated above, these are a very common lead indicator for safety management, but they are also very limited, often nothing more than a measure of how many interactions have been done. There is typically no measure or analysis about whether interactions were done well or whether they have added value to safety management.

It seems universally assumed management interactions around health and safety are a good thing, but are they?

What is their purpose, what are they designed to achieve and how do we know that they are achieving that purpose? Is there a risk that management interactions could be undermining safety in your workplace?

How do you know managers are not just wandering around practising random acts of safety, reinforcing unsafe behaviours and generally just pissing everybody off?

A green traffic light in a health and safety report indicating everybody who should have done a management interaction has done one is misleading and fuels the illusion of safety which underpins so many catastrophic workplace events.

When was the last time anybody provided health and safety reporting that made a meaningful contribution to proving the effectiveness of crucial systems? Have any leaders ever received a report showing a detailed analysis of lifting operations over a 10-month period with a formal, concluded view about the effectiveness of the safety management system to control the risks associated with lifting? What about dropped objects? What about working at height?

What about the efficacy of your permit to work system? Has that ever been analysed and reported on, other than on a case-by-case *"reactive"* basis following an incident?

For your next health and safety *"reporting"* meeting, try this: Scrap your traditional health and safety report, pick a critical risk such as working at heights, and ask your safety manager to provide you with a presentation about whether, or to what extent, the risk has been managed as far as reasonably practicable.

What is your health and safety reporting really telling you, as opposed to the assumptions you choose to make? Is there any evidence that it is proving the effectiveness of your crucial systems?

In my experience, the problems with health and safety reporting and the extent to which it contributes to the Illusion of Safety are a problem of management. If organisations genuinely cared about health and safety management then it is simply not possible for health and safety reporting to look like it does. Health and safety reporting is underscored by unjustified assumptions and a complete lack of challenge of health and safety information.

Earlier, I looked at the Piper Alpha case in the context of systemic failure, specifically the failure of the Permit to Work System. While Piper Alpha does demonstrate systemic failure of crucial process, it also highlights the role of assumption, and a lack of critical thinking, which has infected safety management.

In part, the failure of the Permit to Work system was due to misplaced assumption on the part of management:

> *The managers who had responsibility for the correct operation of the [Permit to Work] system were all aware that the safety personnel on the platform were expected to monitor the daily operation of the system. All of them assumed that because they received no reports of failings the system is working properly. However none of them check the quality of that monitoring nor did they carry out more than the most cursory examination of permits*

when they had occasion to visit Piper. (Cullen, 1990, p. 231)

Many of the observation in the Piper Alpha inquiry were echoed more than 20 years later in the Pike River Royal Commission (Panckhurst, Bell, & Henry, 2012).

In their observation about governance by the Pike River Board, the Royal Commission noted:

> *The board did not verify that effective systems were in place and that risk management was effective. Nor did it properly hold management to account, but instead **assumed that managers would draw the board's attention to any major operational problems**. The board did not provide effective health and safety leadership and protect the workforce from harm. It was distracted by the financial and production pressures that confronted the company.* (my emphasis added) (Panckhurst, Bell, & Henry, 2012, p. 18).

So, where to for safety?

History seems to suggest we have developed a bureaucracy around workplace safety which simultaneously disconnects the workforce from our safety expectations, confuses those expectations to a point where they are not understood by anyone, fails to identify the true state of health and safety in our organisations, at best hides and at worst misleads management about the true state of health and safety in our organisations and to round this all out, management are left with health and safety information which gives no insight into whether the health and safety risks in their business are being managed, but they draw assumptions from lead and lag indicators which have no meaningful connection to workplace reality.

Where do we go?

PART 3
WHERE TO FROM HERE?

MANAGING LEGAL RISK

I n this part of the book, I want to offer some suggestions for how we might move from bureaucracy to clarity and reconnect process with purpose. However, before I can do that, I think it is important to take a little bit of time to discuss the fallacy that bureaucracy manages legal risk. It does not.

In most cases, bureaucracy does not manage legal risk it increases it.

As we have seen in several case studies in this book when an organisation does not comply with its own documented processes, it creates potential legal liability. Bureaucracy only helps to manage legal risk if the bureaucracy represents what is actually happening in practice.

Perhaps a start point for this discussion is to have an honest conversation about how much of what we do in the name of health and safety is actually done in the name of *legal* risk management?

JHAs have been a common thread through this book, and with good reason, because many workers (and managers) see them as an exercise in bureaucracy. As I have previously said, and I will discuss again in the next section, JHAs have a sound theoretical basis to help

Gregory Smith

workers identify, understanding control hazards associated with their work.

But why do we keep them?

Once the work has completed safely, why do organisations invest so much time and effort to collect, collate and store the documents? From a workers' perspective at least, it seems the answer to that question is to protect management from perceived legal risk (Borys, 2009). A manager once explained to me that they kept JHAs so that if a worker made a subsequent workers compensation claim they would *"know what work they were doing on that day"*.

Legal risk management?

My personal reality is, in all the time I have been involved in health and safety, I have never once said to a client that their system of JHA, and all of the historical JHAs they maintained, would be useful to put in front of a regulator or Court.

A very common experience for me when I am involved in fatality investigations is:

- The JHA for the specific job being done at the time of the fatality is poor – it does not identify relevant risks, it is not well written, the risk assessments in the JHA are not valid, along with numerous other issues.

- The explanation for the poor JHA is a *"one-off departure"* – The supervisor who did the JHA is the *"best"* supervisor on the project, is meticulous with their paperwork and always does high-quality JHAs.

- An historical examination of the supervisors JHAs (i.e. six months' worth of JHAs signed by *that* supervisor) reveals all the JHAs are poor, and the same errors in the

JHA which was done for the specific work at the time of the fatality are present in al the JHAs. This is systemic failure.

When this happens, far from helping to manage legal risk, the systemic failure inherent in the JHA process increases legal risk. It creates a picture of an organisation that does not care about, or pay attention to, safety. The argument runs something like this:

If you actually cared about safety, then this critical process – JHA – could not have deteriorated to this level. It would not look like this. The JHA documentation would not be so disconnected from your expectations as described in the JHA processes.

Another curious process which seems to be more concerned about legal risk management than safety is the use of checklists in the workplace.

I think it is a good idea to inspect machinery, plant or equipment before using it to make sure it is safe.

I think, because human beings are fallible and make mistakes, checklists to guide the inspection process are theoretically a good idea. Theoretically, it is a good idea to have a document that sets out what items to check as part of an inspection as a reminder of what to check, or what to look for when you are checking (i.e. what are the indicators that something might be a problem?)

But why do we insist on making workers physically complete a form? Why do we have them tick off a checklist, sign it and submit it? Why do we file it, and then report against how many have been done?

One argument is that the completed checklist is evidence the inspections have been done.

Gregory Smith

History, however, tells us there are two problems with this argument.

First, a completed form is not evidencing an inspection has been done – it is only evidence the form has been *completed.* At best, it is an assumption the inspection has been done.

Second, even if we allow ourselves the luxury of assuming a completed checklist means the inspection has been done, it is not evidence it has been done well, or evidence it has achieved its purpose. It is not proof that hazards have been identified or managed. It provides no more evidence than if the forms were not completed.

If we are honest, it seems the only reason we keep completed checklists is for some ill-informed attempt to manage legal liability. But does this work? What will happen in practice?

Consider the following scenario.

There has been a catastrophic failure of a piece of equipment resulting in the death of a worker. On the face of it, a team of workers had inspected the piece of equipment, they completed a checklist and the piece of equipment had been signed off as safe to use.

Is the checklist evidence the equipment was safe to use when it was signed? Alternatively, is the failure of the piece of equipment evidence the workers lied when they signed off the checklist?

In practice, the workers will have to explain what they checked, how they checked it and how they formed the view the equipment was safe use. Their evidence – what they say – will be tested against the objective evidence. In other words, how likely is it the workers' version of events is true, based on what we know about the event?

In this context the question of whether the workers have completed a checklist is irrelevant to the question whether the worker made an informed decision about the safety or serviceability of the equipment.

If the checklist has been marked as "*safe*", and objectively the equipment was not safe this does not, of itself, protect an organisation. For example, if the worker's evidence demonstrates they are not qualified or competent to make the assessments required by the checklist, then the employer will have to defend the worker's level of competence. The checklist is irrelevant.

If the worker's evidence is, they routinely completed the checklist as a tick and flick exercise, the employer will have to defend how that systemic failure was allowed to develop. The checklist is irrelevant.

What about a long history of completed checklists?

What if a piece of equipment is checked every day for six months, and signed off a safe? Again, the completed checklists really add no value. It is the same inquiry – what do the workers say? What is the objective evidence? If the objective evidence shows that the piece of equipment has been unsafe for a long period of time, but checklists have routinely been signed off as safe, again the employer will have to defend how the systemic failure developed. In this case, the completed checklists are worse than irrelevant they provide positive evidence of the employer's failure to adequately monitor their own systems of work.

So, if part of providing a safe workplace means inspecting plant and equipment, how do we know if things are being checked?

Well to start, that is the wrong question. We really should not be that interested in whether things are being "*checked*". If we are talking about plant, machinery and equipment checklists what we are interested in – or what we should be interested in – is whether the worker understands how to operate the equipment. Whether they understand the hazards associated with the equipment. Whether they can identify if the appropriate controls are in place to manage those hazards. If they can identify if there are any faults or problems with the equipment.

The fact that a "*check*" has been done is irrelevant. The issues we are concerned with go to understanding and competence.

So how do we get assurance about those things?

Well, the obvious answer to that is, we go and look.

And by "*we*" I mean a subject matter expert.

There is no point in me going to have a conversation with an operator about a pre-start inspection on a front-end loader. I know nothing about the safe operation of front-end loaders, or whether there is a problem with a front-end loader. I would add nothing to the conversation and could do nothing but agree with and reinforce what the operator tells me – which may or may not be correct.

Ideally a subject matter expert should go into the workplace. The subject matter expert would ask the worker whether they have done their pre-start inspection and then redo the pre start inspection with the worker, having them tell the subject matter expert how they did the pre-start inspection and all of the things that they did to determine whether or not the equipment was safe to operate.

If that conversation is consistent with the subject matter expert's expectations, then we can start to build a picture and have some confidence about the workers competence and understanding. If the worker's statements are wholly inconsistent with the expectations of the subject matter expert, then we are starting to see a different picture emerge.

The job of the subject matter expert is to report back to the organisation on a regular basis about the efficacy of the inspection process.

Of course, you can argue that this process is just as liable to corruption as the whole checklist process itself. There is nothing to prevent a subject matter expert turning their process of review into a tick and flick exercise. But in my view, a subject matter expert who has personal responsibility to report back on the efficacy of the process is likely to be far more diligent than individual workers who are confronted with repetitive, daily checklists which are often an impediment to getting on with work. Moreover, from a legal risk management perspective regular updates from a subject matter expert are far better evidence of due diligence and management oversight of safety than a monthly report with a green traffic light saying 100% of checklists have been completed.

I accept that there are layers of competence necessary to move an organisation in this direction. Subject matter experts need to have training in workplace interactions and conversations. Managers need training and understanding about due diligence and how to critically assess health and safety reports. Overall, an effective approach to managing legal risk in the context of health and safety requires far more effort and organisation than the simplistic *"paper safe"* approach which characterises modern safety management. However, this approach, in my view has far greater connection with purpose than what we currently see in workplaces.

146

Gregory Smith

UNDERSTAND IF YOUR SYSTEMS ARE USEFUL

I think it is a damning indictment on the health and safety industry that inquiry after inquiry reveals documented safety management systems are not understood by the workforce and are of little relevance to their day-to-day work. It seems to me to be the pinnacle of failed due diligence if this disconnect between management and workers goes unrecognised until somebody dies. It is so easily revealed by having a genuine conversation with the workers.

It can only be true that a meaningful move from bureaucracy to clarity will occur with the involvement of the workforce. A connection between process and purpose will only be achieved if management is prepared to have a genuine, meaningful discussion with workers to understand if they find health and safety processes helpful. Indeed, a growing consensus would suggest the best way to develop safety management systems is to have the workforce tell management how they actually do the job, and management simply adopt and reflect the workforces lived experience as part of the process.

In my experience, a significant cause of bureaucracy in safety management is that safety is management driven. Safety is the product of management devising the best theoretical, management

147

model to manage hazards in the workplace. Organisations will not break the bureaucratic cycle by employing the same management and management strategies to look at the problem. I think the worst possible outcome of the concepts I have articulated in this book would be for management to develop a project team to look at health and safety bureaucracy. Management teams will not deal with bureaucracy, they will simply create a different version of it.

Learn the lessons from this book and adopt some of my strategies, by all means. But do not think they are right. Do not think they will work in your organisation. Everything I offer in this book is subject to the Safety Paradox, just as everything which has gone before it.

Health and safety should hand control back to the workers, and simply act as the scribe.

Gregory Smith

CONNECTION WITH PURPOSE

I started out by describing bureaucracy as a disconnection between process and purpose, and many of the examples used in this book reinforce that definition.

There are many factors in safety management that contribute to safe workplaces, which have nothing to do with process. Basic principles around commitment to safety, the ability of people to have meaningful conversations in the workplace, genuine care about people, and a range of other factors that safety experts, psychologists, sociologists and others are far better place than I to talk about.

However, process is important. Process is important, if for no other reason than safety management is dominated by it, and until we find a way to control process it will continue to impede our ability to create work environments which give safety the best opportunity of success.

So how might we move to a more purpose driven view of safety, and use this view to reduce bureaucracy?

What is the purpose?

I think the start point is to critically think about health and safety processes, and ask:

- What is the purpose of the process; and

- How does the process contribute to the purpose?

Earlier in the book I described a whole range of processes that were connected to the JHA. If the purpose of the JHA is to help workers identify the hazards associated with their work, understand how to manage those hazards and to ensure a common understanding of the hazards and how they will be managed, how does the process associated with the JHA contribute to that purpose?

At the most basic level, how does documenting that process and requiring workers to sign on to the documentation contribute to the purpose? Is it possible that the process detracts from the purpose (i.e. the Safety Paradox)?

Remember, evidencing the process is not the same thing as achieving the purpose. We need to extract from our processes those parts of the process which are designed to achieve the purpose and those parts of the process that are designed as evidence.

In some cases, achievement of purpose and creation of evidence can be the same thing. It is at least arguable that the JHA form is designed to achieve the purpose, because it provides the framework within which the conversation about hazards and how they are managed can happen. At the same time the JHA form can be used as evidence. But if we were solely concerned with the achievement of purpose what changes might we make to the JHA form?

Would we ask workers to sign it?

150

Gregory Smith

Would we keep it?

Would we review the JHA during a management inspection, or would we just have conversations with workers about hazards and how they might be managed?

What do we want evidence of?

If we can strip our processes back only to those elements which make a meaningful contribution to purpose, then we can have a conversation about evidence. But evidence also needs to relate to purpose.

As I have repeatedly said in this book, a lot of safety bureaucracy is done in the name of measuring activity. Many of the core health and safety obligations we impose on workers are nothing more than data collection to demonstrate activity.

Evidence of activity is meaningless. It provides no proof that safety is being managed effectively. It provides no support for managing legal risk.

Both safety and legal risk management require evidence of purpose.

As I discussed earlier in the context of checklists, evidence of purpose requires a conscious effort to understand the purpose of a process, and specifically check against that purpose.

As an example, I have worked with a construction organisation that wanted to try and get some meaningful insight into safety. Working with them, we identified that one of their "*crucial systems*" (to borrow from the Pike River Royal Commission) was "*supervision*".

Working with the client we identified that the markers of good supervision, in the context of safety and health, were:

- Workers would understand the tasks they were performing;

- Workers would understand the hazards associated with those tasks;

- Workers would understand how those hazards were meant to be controlled; and

- The understanding of tasks, hazards and controls would be consistent across all of the workers.

If those markers of supervision were present, management could have a high degree of confidence that supervision on-the-job was consistent with the organisation's expectations.

The way the process was tested in practice was for senior management to go to site, with a subject matter expert, and have conversations with the workers. However, the conversations with the workers were not general, they were one-on-one – each manager speaking to a single worker – and they were targeted. The conversations were designed to get an understanding of the workers knowledge about the task, the hazards and the controls.

After the infield conversations, the management team would come together and discuss what they had been told. If the individual conversations from all of the workers were consistent managers had confidence in the level of supervision. If the conversations were not consistent, this was a marker of problematic supervision. It suggested that supervisors were not ensuring the same message was being distributed amongst, and understood by, all workers.

Gregory Smith

Beyond that, the subject matter expert assessed the conversations. While workers might be able to tell us about the hazards and how they are meant to be controlled, the subject matter expert was able to tell us whether they were the "*right*" hazards and controls. The management team were not experts. The management team could have conversations with the workers and compare those conversations to understand consistency, but they were not experts to know whether the workers were doing the correct thing.

This was a process designed to give assurance of purpose. Was site supervision achieving the purpose it was designed for?

To reinforce some of the messages we also reviewed the conversations against paperwork. Having created a picture of what the workers understood about hazards and how they were meant to be controlled, we compared that to the front-line health and safety documentation, typically JHAs and Safe Work Method Statements. Importantly it was conversation first, paperwork second. Typically, management interactions start with the paperwork, emphasising the importance of the paperwork over the conversation.

What the management team found most disconcerting was the extent to which workers understood their work, the hazards and the controls and the extent to which the workers understanding was correct, as confirmed by the subject matter expert, but that the work, the hazards and the controls were not reflected in the JHA. What added to their discomfort was when we took the document review back a step to the documented policies and procedures. That examination revealed that what was documented in the JHA was not consistent with what was described in the document policies and procedures, and the workers understanding of the hazards and controls while "*safe*", was not consistent with the documented policies and procedures.

153

For the management team this exercise really highlighted the gap between the systems as they imagined them and what was happening in practice. It further highlighted the disconnect between the actual state of work as it was performed compared to the information they received in their monthly health and safety management reports which were dominated by green traffic lights.

Gregory Smith

CRITICALLY QUESTION HEALTH AND SAFETY REPORTS

O
ne of the most disconcerting issues I continued to deal with professionally is the failure of health and safety reporting to add value to our understanding of health and safety risk. Typically, I see this in the context of legal proceedings: a fatality has occurred, a regulator is investigating, I am trying to establish evidence that my client was managing risks as low as reasonably practicable – but the evidence does not exist.

Health and safety reporting in organisations simply does not provide any narrative statement about whether health and safety generally is being well managed, or whether specific critical risks are being well managed.

The case studies in this book are consistent. Injury rate data and so-called "*lead indicators*" are not evidence that health and safety hazards are being managed. They are not evidence that the organisation is managing those hazards as low as reasonably practicable. They are not evidence of due diligence.

More often than not, health and safety reporting provides a misleading picture of the true state of health and safety in the organisation and contributes to the Illusion of Safety.

Management should consistently and robustly challenge health and safety reports.

If you are concerned about the quality of supervision in your organisation, you should ask for an analysis and a written report about the quality and effectiveness of supervision.

If you are concerned about the efficacy of change management in your organisation, you should ask for an analysis and a written report about how well change is managed.

If you are concerned about hazards associated with working at height in your organisation, you should ask for an analysis and a written report about how well work at height is managed.

You should not accept that low injury rates means your critical risks are being managed. You should not accept that green traffic lights in your monthly health and safety report mean critical controls are working effectively.

The lack of critical thinking about health and safety reporting is easy to test in your organisation. First, ask yourself what you are concerned about, or simply pick a critical health and safety hazard in your organisation. Look at the health and safety information you have received over the last six months. Consider reports, briefings, meetings you have attended, site visits you have conducted – anything that provides some level of information about health and safety in your organisation. Then ask yourself the question, what does all that information tell me about my concern?

Does it tell me if my concern is well managed?

Gregory Smith

Does it tell me if my concern is being managed in accordance with the documented safety management system?

Does it tell me if the workforce understands our expectations in relation to the concern?

If it does not, if all of the activity around health and safety you have participated in, or information you have received in the last six months cannot answer basic questions about whether your health and safety concerns are being managed, then what is the point?

INCIDENT INVESTIGATIONS

While I have been critical of incident investigations and the extent to which they have become bureaucratised, there is no doubt that incident investigations, properly done, are one of the best avenues organisations have to understand the true state of their safety management systems.

To contribute to our understanding and management of bureaucracy in safety, incident investigations need to be conscious of it. Incident investigations need to be directed to, and purposefully challenge, bureaucracy.

Some critical questions that should be included in incident investigations to help uncover bureaucracy include:

- What safety management processes applied to the management of this hazard?

- What was the purpose of each safety management process and how is that evidenced? Do we even say what the purpose is?

158

- What evidence is there that the purpose of each safety management process was being achieved, *prior to the incident*?

- Was there a "*proper*" system to manage the hazards identified in this incident?

- Was there "*adequate*" supervision to know if the system was in place and effective?

- Prior to the incident, what did the organisation know about how well the hazards were or were not managed?

- Was this a one-off departure from our safety management system, or is there any evidence that it was a systemic failure? Had this behaviour become normalised?

- Did the:

  - Workers involved in this incident; and

  - Workers generally,

  Understand the requirements of the safety management system in relation to this hazard?

Is also worth considering that incident investigations do not have to be limited to "*incidents*". There is absolutely nothing to prevent an organisation investigating work as it is normally performed. In other words, there is nothing to prevent an organisation going into the field, stopping a work activity and reviewing that work activity as though an incident had occurred. All of the questions I have described above can be asked about work as it is being performed whether or not there has been an incident. Indeed, I would argue that these proactive, "*no incident*" investigations offer more value than many of the minor incident investigations organisations undertake.

In my experience a *"no incident"* investigation often reveals the same gaps in safety management system (i.e. poor documentation, lack of worker understanding etc.) that is revealed after a serious accident. The difference between *"safe"* work and accidents seems to have nothing to do with our systems of safety management. The quality of safety management seems to be the same in both cases.

Gregory Smith

FINAL THOUGHTS

I do not know how it happened. I am not sure how we got here. I am sure that regulators, lawyers, the insurance industry and others all had a role to play, but somehow safety has shifted.

Somehow, safety went from being part of what a business did, to a self-perpetuating industry. An industry that sells products, technology, concepts, theories – all of which seem to move progressively further and further away from the intended outcome. Providing safe workplaces.

Rather than build a relationship between workers and management, safety has become a wedge. Safety has become a byword for meddling, incompetence and distrust. The safety industry has lost its key stakeholder – the worker.

The objective of health and safety management seems, to me, self-evident – to provide an environment that minimises harm to workers and other stakeholders affected by the conduct of our business. Anything which potentially compromises that objective needs critical scrutiny, not blind adoption as the next good idea.

If this book has offended anybody, it was not my intention. My intention was simply to highlight my concerns, formulated over the last 30 years of picking up the pieces of failed safety management.

I do not pretend to have all the answers. I may not have any useful answers at all. But if all this book does is cause organisations to critically question their processes, and the impact those processes have on the workers, and go and seek their own answers, then that is enough.

Gregory Smith

References

Baker, J. A., Leveson, N., Bowman, F. L., Priest, S., Erwin, G., Rosenthal, I., . . . Wilson, L. D. (2007). *The Report of the BP U.S. Refineries Independent Safety Review Panel.* Retrieved December 24, 2017, from http://www.csb.gov/assets/1/19/Baker_panel_report1.pdf

Borthwick, D. (2010). *Report of the Montara Commission of Inquiry.* Canberra: Commonwealth of Australia.

Borys, D. (2009). Exploring risk awareness as a cultural approach to safety: Exposing teh gap between work as imagined and work as actually performed. *Safety Science Monitor, 13*(2), 1 - 11.

Columbia Accident Investigation Board. (2003). *Report Volume 1.* Washington D.C.: National Aeronautics and Space Administration.

Cullen, L. (1990). *The Public Enquiry into the Piper Alpha Disaster.* London: HMSO.

Dawson, S. M., & Brooks, B. J. (1999). *The Esso Longford Gas Plant Accident: Report of the Longford Royal Commission.* Melbourne: Parliament of Victoria.

Dekker, S. (2008). Chronicling the Emergence of Confused Consensus. In E. Hollnagel, D. D. Woods, & N. Leveson, *Resilience Engineering: Concepts and Precepts* (pp. 77 - 92). Aldershot: Ashgate.

Dekker, S. (2015). *Safety Differently: Human Factors for a New Era.* Boca Raton: CRC Press.

Gregory Smith

Education and Health Standing Committee. (2014). *Shining a Light on FIFO Mental Health: A Discussion Paper.* Legislative Assembly. Perth: Parliament of Western Australia. Retrieved January 14, 2018, from http://www.parliament.wa.gov.au/publications/tabledpapers. nsf/displaypaper/3912437aa3442764c122634f48257d9d003 3d216/$file/2437.pdf

Education and Health Standing Committee. (2015). *The impact of FIFO work practices on mental health: Final Report.* Legislative Assembly. Perth: Parliament of Western Australia.

Haddon-Cave. (2009). *And Independent Review into the broader issues surrounding the loss of RAF Nimrod MR2 Aircraft XV203 in Afghanistan in 2006.* London: The Stationery Office Limited.

Hale, A. R., Heijer, T., & Koornneef, F. (2003). Management of safety rules: The case of railways. *Safety Science Monitor, 7*(1), 1-11.

Hillman v Ferro Con (SA) Pty Ltd (in Liquidation) and Anor [2013] SAIRC 22.

Hollnagel, E., Woods, d. D., & Leveson, N. (2008). *Resilience Engineering Concepts and Precepts.* Aldershot: Ashgate Publishing Limited.

Hopkins, A. (2004). *Safety, Culture and Risk: The Organisational Causes of Disasters.* Sydney: CCH.

Inquest into the death of Cameron Brandt Cole, 2009/17777 (Queensland Coroner's Court September 11, 2015).

International Nuclear Safety Advisory Group. (1986). *Summary Report on the Post Accident Review Meeting on the Chernobyl Accident. Safety Series No. 75. INSAG-1.* Vienna: International Atomic Energy Agency.

International Nuclear Safety Advisory Group. (1992). *The Chernobyl Accident: Updating of INSAG-1, INSAG-7.* Vienna: International Atomic Energy Agency.

Kletz, T. (2001). *Learning from Accidents.* Oxford: Gulf Professional Publishing.

Lynn, J., & Jay, A. (1984). *The Compleat Yes Minister.* London: British Broadcasting Corporation.

Non-inquest findings into the deaths of Jamie Christopher ADAMS and Gary Robert WATKINS, 2007/136 and 2007/135 (Queensland Coroner's Court January 19, 2018).

Panckhurst, H., Bell, S., & Henry, D. (2012). *Royal Commission on the Pike River Coal Mine Tragedy - Volume 2.* Wellington: Pike River Royal Commission. Retrieved December 24, 2017, from http://pikeriver.royalcommission.govt.nz/vwluResources/Final-Report-Volume-Two/$file/ReportVol2-whole.pdf

Provan, D. J., Dekker, S. W., & Rae, A. J. (2017). Bureaucracy, influence and beliefs: A literature review of the factors shaping the role of a safety professional. *Safety Science, 98,* 98 - 112.

Rebbit, D., & Erickson, J. (2016). Hypercompliance: Too much of a good thing? *Professional Safety*, 31-37.

Rittel, H. W., & Webber, M. M. (1973). Dilemmas in a General Theory of Planning. *Policy Sciences*(4), 155 - 169.

Gregory Smith

Safe Work (NSW) v Action Concreting and Constructions Pty Ltd [2017] NSWDC 191.

Sellenger Centre for Research in Law, Justice and Social Change. (2013). *FIFO/DIDO Mental Health Research Report 2013*. Perth: Lifeline WA.

Sheen, H. (1987). *MV Herald of Free Enterprise: Report of Court No. 8074 Formal Investigation.* London: Her Majesty's Stationery Office.

Smith, G. (2016). *Management Obligations for Health and Safety.* Boca Raton: CRC Press.

(2012, February 13). Transcript of Phase Three Hearing Commencing 13 February 2012 at Greymouth. Greymouth, New Zealand: Pike River Royal Commission. Retrieved December 24, 2017, from http://pikeriver.royalcommission.govt.nz/Phase-3-Hearing-Transcripts

U.S. Chemical Safety and Hazard Investigation Board. (2007). *Investigation Report. Refinery Explosion and Fire BP Texas City.* Texac City: U.S. Chemical Safety and Hazard Investigation Board.

Workcover Authority of New Sout Wales (Inspector Byer) v Cleary Bros (Bombo) Pty Ltd, [2001] NSWIRComm 278 (New South Wales Industrial Relations Commission 2001).

Index

assumption, 38, 41, 125, 141, 148

audit, 79, 89, 90, 103

Baiada Poultry, 9

Baker Panel, 98, 99, 125

Baker Panel Review, 125

BP Texas City, 55, 75, 115, 125

case citations, 13

case studies, 7, 12, 18, 19, 145, 161

checklist, 16, 40, 47, 115, 116, 117, 119, 121, 126, 147, 148, 149, 151

Comcare v John Holland, 90

competence, 29, 77, 95, 96, 97, 98, 99, 150, 151

complexity, 4, 26, 27, 48, 49, 86

Cyclone George, 20

DPP v Vibro-Pile (Aust) Pty Ltd, 10

due diligence, 68, 151, 153, 161

Esso, 72, 73, 74, 85

Ferro Con, 102, 103, 105

fly in/fly out work, 57

frontline risk assessment, 39, 40, 109, 139

Fry v Keating, 31, 69

golden rules, 50, 51

Harris v Coles Supermarkets Australia Pty Ltd, 30, 127

health and safety reporting, 14, 122, 136, 138, 140, 141, 161, 162

Herald of Free Enterprise, 37

Holmes v Re Spence & Co Pty Ltd, 9, 18

illusion of safety, 15, 60, 61, 65, 104, 122, 137, 140

Illusion of Safety, 17, 92, 93, 138, 141, 162

incident investigation models, 124

incident investigations, 123, 124, 127, 128, 129, 130, 132, 134, 164, 165

initiative overload, 15, 55, 56, 57, 61, 75, 112

injury rates, 14, 136, 137, 162

Inspector Davies v Prospect Electricity, 18

Inspector McCarthy (nee Shaw) v Siva & Jeya Pty Ltd, 82

Inspector Shepherd v Desiya Pty Ltd, 31

JHA, 39, 103, 104, 105, 109, 110, 116, 117, 120, 139, 145, 146, 147, 156, 157, 159

Key Performance Indicator, 25, 40

Kirwin v Laing O'Rourke (BMC) Pty Ltd, 21

Laing O'Rourke (BMC) Pty Ltd v Kirwin, 9, 18, 21

legal risk, 26, 80, 81, 87, 127, 139, 145, 146, 147, 151, 157

Model Work Health and Safety Act, 29

Moore v SD Tillett Memorials, 31

paperwork, 28, 37, 38, 39, 56, 74, 80, 101, 102, 104, 112, 117, 120, 146, 159

Permit to Work, 39, 50, 68, 141

Pike River, 76, 130, 132, 142, 157

Piper Alpha, 68, 141, 142

procedure, 19, 40, 47, 49, 57, 81, 85, 86, 87, 108, 109, 114, 116, 128

procedures, 3, 39, 49, 51, 56, 57, 60, 65, 74, 76, 77, 78, 80, 81, 83, 85, 106, 107, 110, 114, 115, 124, 127, 128, 159

prosecution, 8, 9, 10, 11, 12, 18, 19, 21, 45, 72, 80, 113

RAF Nimrod XV230, 3

Royal Commission, 72, 73, 74, 76, 85, 130, 134, 142, 157

Rules, 16, 27, 34, 35, 62

Safe Work Method Statements, 110, 112, 113, 159

Safe Work NSW v Wollongong Glass, 31, 67, 112

safety differently, 42

safety initiatives, 5, 17, 50, 54, 55, 57, 61

Safety Paradox, 17, 46, 50, 54, 55, 61, 74, 92, 125, 138, 139, 154, 156

Seage v State of New South Wales, 44

Slivak v Lurgi (Australia) Pty Ltd, 18

supervision, 11, 17, 18, 21, 29, 61, 113, 157, 158, 159, 162, 165

Take 5, 39, 118, 119, 120, 121, 122, 138

Texas City, 98, 172

traffic light, 25, 26, 122, 140, 151

training, 19, 29, 30, 31, 40, 47, 50, 62, 81, 87, 95, 96, 97, 98, 99, 113, 115, 123, 128, 130, 151

Transpacific Industrial Solutions Pty Limited v Phelps, 43

trivial, 14, 15, 16, 27, 28, 35, 42, 43, 44, 47, 110

US Chemical Safety and Hazard Investigation Board, 91

wicked problem, 48

Workcover Authority of New South Wales (Inspector

Byer) v *Cleary Bros (Bombo)* Pty Ltd, 10